If You Love Me, Don't Love Me

If You Love Me,
Don't Love Me

Constructions of Reality
and Change
in Family Therapy

Mony Elkaïm, M.D.

Translated by Hendon Chubb, Ph.D.

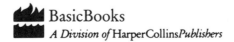

BasicBooks
A Division of HarperCollins*Publishers*

The poetry of Homer quoted on page 157 is from *The Myth of Sisyphus and Other Essays* by Justin O'Brien. Copyright © 1955 by Alfred A. Knopf, Inc. Reprinted by permission of the publisher.

Library of Congress Cataloging-in-Publication Data
Elkaïm, Mony.
   [Si tu m'aimes, ne m'aime pas. English]
   If you love me, don't love me: constructions of reality and change in family therapy/Mony Elkaïm; translated by Hendon Chubb.
        p.   cm.
   Translation of: Si tu m'aimes, ne m'aime pas. Editions de Seuil, Paris, 1989.
   Includes bibliographical references.
   ISBN 0–465–03206–0
   1. Family psychotherapy.   I. Title.
RC488.5.E3513   1990   90–80677
616.89'156—dc20   CIP

To the memory of my father

Contents

✿

Foreword

> *The observer cannot exist outside the observed system.*
> —Mony Elkaïm

ARISTOTLE, if he were a reader in a publishing house, would have rejected a book entitled *If You Love Me, Don't Love Me* for its logical absurdity. Descartes may have recognized an intent in this fallacy and rejected it as a sign of malice. I guess Kant would have taken this ill-constructed inference not too seriously, and might have dismissed it as a harmless paralogism, while Russell would have prohibited its construction, for it violates his Theory of Types. However, progressive semioticists would argue that in this phrase the two like verbs "love," signify two unlike functions: "love$_1$" and "love$_2$." Thus, the apparent semantic clash in the title does not exist: *If You Love$_1$ Me, Don't Love$_2$ Me.* Such a device may have satisfied Aristotle, Descartes, Kant, Russell, and others, but certainly it misses the point the author of this book intends to make, not only with its title, but through the entire book.

What Elkaïm wants to do is force us to see ourselves as part of the universe or, better, the universe as part of ourselves. That is, he wants us to think in terms that are "inclusive," "contextual," "participatory," "connected," "integral," "involved," "circular causal," "mutually dependent," "together," "dialogical," and so on. There is very little in the tradition of

Western thought on which the author could have built his system, for the central effort of this tradition is to extricate oneself from involvement in order to escape the accusation of having a personal view. "Objectivity" is the name of the game that absolves us from responsibility: the properties of the observer shall not enter the description of his observations.

Spinoza, however, would have sympathized with our author, since he himself wrestled with the logic of a system that contains its own creator. "How, then, can one think himself inside the system without surrendering the possibility of judging it in terms other than its own?" asks a Spinoza scholar[1]. Spinoza's answer is a *reductio ad absurdum* of a stipulated "outsider" by invoking his celebrated worm:

Suppose that a parasitic worm living in the bloodstream tried to make sense of its surroundings: from the point of view of the worm, each drop of blood would appear as an independent whole and not as a part of a total system. . . . But in fact, the nature of the blood can be understood only in the context of a larger system in which blood, lymph and other fluids interact; and this system in turn is a part of a still larger whole. If we men begin with the bodies that surround us in nature and treat them as independent wholes . . . then we shall be in error precisely as the worm is in error. We must grasp the system as a whole before we can hope to grasp the nature of the part, since the nature of the part is determined by its role in the total system.

O.K! But how can we avoid the worm's fallacy? We do it by seeing the fallacy of the question. Since we are part of the universe, the only way to judge it is in its own terms. There is no other way. Russell's hope to escape the *coincidentia oppositorum*, the paradox, by distinguishing between language,

---

[1] A. MacIntyre: "Spinoza, Benedict (Baruch)," in *The Encyclopedia of Philosophy* (New York: Macmillan, 1967), 7, 532–41.

and language about language, a meta-language; a language about language and a language about language about language, a meta-meta-language, and up and up the seductive hierarchical ladder, is only postponing the moment of truth when it is realized that it is in language that we speak about language, that is, that language always speaks about itself. In what way?

In its appearance, language seems to be denotative, monologing about things in the world. In its function, however, it is connotative, appealing to concepts in the semantic repertoire of the other's mind. If this is so, how can we avoid the destructive forces of the contradictions, the paradoxes, the semantic clashes? We cannot and we should not, for these are not destructive but *con*structive forces indeed, as Mony Elkaïm demonstrates on almost every page of his book or, better, at every consultation in which people come to seek his help. Since he chooses to let the only medicine at his disposal be language, he uses the intrinsic tensions of language, the contrarieties, to break through the dead ends of semantic traps.

"What brought it about that you invented this therapeutic strategy?" I asked him once.
"As a kid I was living on a street that divided two hostile factions of the town. I listened to both. I learned from both. And then I came to the conclusion: They both were right!"
"But with one of them must have been the truth!" I said, and he replied:
"The problem is not truth, it is peace!"

What this book is about is how to transcend "truth" and to enter the domain of "peace."

—HEINZ VON FOERSTER
Pescadero, February 1990.

Foreword

Everybody who has seen Mony Elkaïm at work—either in
an actual clinical setting or while demonstrating his approach
in a simulated family session—has probably come away with
the same question in mind: How does he do it? How does he
manage to gather a wealth of information from a single inter-
change or, conversely, what enables him to distill out of the
chaotic complexity of a family's interaction those elements on
which he then bases his surprisingly effective interventions?

In this book, Dr. Elkaïm shows that his ability is not the
result of a vague, esoteric gift beyond rational description like
"intuition," but rather the expression of a combination of solid
clinical experience and a wide range of other practical, scientific, and, above all, epistemological interests and studies.
His international background and his exposure to different
cultures and social milieus give further depth to his approaches to human problems.

This book could hardly be published at a more timely moment. What we are now witnessing in the field of family therapy is more and more criticism of systems theory because of
unfamiliarity with or oversimplification of its basic concepts.
People clamor for a "return to the individual" and the richness of our "inner" world; they see the systemic approach as
"mechanistic," "devoid of feeling," blind to the importance of
the past, and so on. Mony Elkaïm, one of the main exponents

of the application of systems theory to social phenomena, manages to show that these contradictions and irreconcilabilities do not exist. On the strength of practical examples he demonstrates that he does not sit "above" the family system as an "objective" observer, but rather studies the "realities" constructed by the family-plus-therapist system, their ethical implications and their potential for change. These may seem very difficult subjects, but Dr. Elkaïm presents them in simple and often humorous language and by means of very explicit, practical examples from his work.

It is a pleasure and an honor for me to introduce Mony Elkaïm's book to the Anglo-American reader. I wish it the same success it has had in Europe.

—Paul Watzlawick
Palo Alto, May 1990

Acknowledgments

FIRST of all, I would like to thank Jean-Luc Giribone who gave me the opportunity to write the French version of this book and who, chapter after chapter, generously offered me his help and his advice.

My thanks also go to Jo Ann Miller and Lynn Hoffman who assisted me in writing the American version of this book which differs in many respects from the original version. They were helped in this by Hendon Chubb who, in addition to translating this book, suggested numerous improvements and helped me carry them out.

I am also grateful to those who helped me to finalize the manuscript: Esther Cohen, Judith Good, Francesca Rona, and Susan Zurn.

I would like to express my appreciation to those persons whose work influenced this book, particularly Robert Castel, Félix Guattari, Emmanuel Levinas, Humberto Maturana, Ilya Prigogine, Francisco Varela, and Heinz von Foerster.

Félix Guattari, Francisco Varela and Heinz von Foerster were kind enough to read parts of the manuscript and offer their suggestions. I am grateful to them just as I am grateful to Yvonne Bonner, Julien Mendlewicz, Solana Orlando, and Colette Simonet whose comments allowed me to clarify the contents of this book.

I am indebted to those who initiated me into the various

facets of the psychotherapeutic field: Christian Beels, Harris Peck, Al Scheflen, and Israel Zwerling.

Finally, I would like to thank my co-workers at the Institute for Family and Human Systems Studies: Chantale Dermine, Edith Goldbeter, Alain Marteaux, Martine Nibelle, Geneviève Platteau, and Jacques Pluymaekers; my colleagues at the psychiatry department of the Erasmus Hospital and in particular, Dominique Pardoen; as well as my patients and students without whom this book would not have existed.

Introduction

IN recent years many questions have been raised about the theoretical framework of systemic family therapy. Certainly the field can claim to have made a major epistemological break with the linear approach that has been traditional in mental health—by refusing to see the individual as the source and locus of problems, by studying the context in which a symptom appears, by calling into question the notion of cause and effect and the idea that the individual is the slave of the past. Even so, the success of family therapy seems to have more to do with the richness of its interventions than with the impressiveness of its constructs. In this book I will discuss on both the clinical and the theoretical level two major problems that confront practitioners in the field.

Stability and Change

Most systemic therapies draw their basic assumptions from the general system theory of Ludwig von Bertalanffy. Bertalanffy's theory, being concerned with the behavior of open systems that are in equilibrium, deals more with stability than with change. It focuses on general laws and assigns a minimal role to history.

Family therapists who work from these assumptions are interested in general laws that apply to all families and concentrate their clinical attention, at least in principle, on the here and now. They deal with families as if they were playing a game of chess, where there is no need to know the history of the game to understand the situation at a given moment. In spite of the fact that therapy is concerned with change and what is unique and different in people, the intellectual foundation of much traditional family therapy is concerned with stability and general laws.

General system theory has certainly rendered great services to the family therapy movement. For example, thinking that a symptom can have the function of keeping a human system in a state of equilibrium has proved to be extremely fruitful on the clinical level. But therapists have begun to feel more and more uncomfortable with its limitations. Their work is far richer than their theory.

One of the major aims of this book is to address the limitations of general system theory as applied to family therapy. Inspired by the work of Ilya Prigogine, a Nobel laureate in chemistry, on systems in the process of change (which Prigogine calls "systems far from equilibrium"), I attach great importance to the special rules of each system, to *singularities*, which are elements specific to the particular system, to chance, and to history.

However, history for me is neither linear nor determining. A person's life is not subject to a mechanical repetition because of some past trauma. Historical factors are necessary for the explanation of current problems, but not sufficient. It is the operation of these elements *in the context of the therapeutic system* of which we are part that determines whether symptoms stay the same, get worse, improve, or disappear. In addition, the future of a system can be totally changed by the amplification of some apparently trivial element in the current situation.

As I develop this theme, I will flesh out my theoretical discussion with concrete examples, in order to provide clinical tools for therapists who want to respect what is unique in their patients and themselves, and to open up options for the families they are seeing.

Self-reference

A second problem that confronts systemic therapists is self-reference. In chapter 3, I describe how a journalist once asked the French writer Raymond Aron, who was in London at the time of the French Occupation, how he could have remained unaware of Hitler's extermination of the Jews. Aron replied that he could imagine the concentration camps and the forced labor but had been unable to conceive of the "industrial" extermination taking place, in spite of what he was reading in the underground press. What he could not conceive of simply did not exist.

We cannot perceive reality as an objective truth; we construct our personal version of reality. We cannot separate ourselves from the situation we are describing. How is this important in therapy? Let us take an example from a case I discuss in chapter 4. A patient is complaining that her husband does not choose her over other women, but at the same time she is afraid of being chosen. When she was a child, her parents preferred her sisters to her: she wants to be chosen but cannot believe that this is possible. Being chosen is also an issue for the therapist, who associates it with catastrophe. Her father, who loved her and preferred her to the other members of the family, died when she was six. Since the therapist too is afraid of being chosen, there is a danger that the therapist and client will validate each other's views and cooperate to conduct the therapy in a way that avoids change.

It is difficult for all of us, including therapists, to differentiate between what is outside of us and what is a part of us. In the systemic model, what the therapist experiences can be seen as a result of self-reference. Under the shelter of Whitehead and Russell's work on paradoxes, as interpreted by Bateson, traditional systemic therapists have treated the self-referential paradox as a sophism; this is interesting philosophy, but it scarcely tells us what to do with the phenomenon itself. This way of dealing with self-reference is in line with traditional thinking in the experimental sciences: the characteristics of the observer must not contaminate what is being studied. In my opinion it is not possible to speak of a human relationship as if the observer were not part of the situation being described; but what the therapist feels relates not only to his or her personal history but also to the system in which the feelings emerge.

In this book I attempt to show you how to work from within the self-referential paradox rather than trying to escape it. The meaning and function of the therapist's feelings in the context of the therapeutic system are the tools both for understanding the system and for intervening in it.

A New Model

What I propose is a new model for couple and family therapy, based on my attempt to take a fresh look at the two problems I have sketched. The model approaches time and history in a different way, attends to the singularities of the systems the therapist is involved in, and helps the therapist to see his or her own feelings, as well as the feelings of the family members, as tools for change.

The model uses the notion of reciprocal double binds; two persons, part of the same system, ask for something that they are not prepared to accept as possible. As an example, let us look at the husband in a couple. Suppose he wants his wife to love him but at the same time he fears that love is always followed by abandonment. On the verbal level he will say, "Love me," but on the nonverbal level he will be saying, "Don't love me." Then whatever the wife does to satisfy one of the demands will be unsatisfactory because it addresses only one level of the double bind.

But for such a pattern to continue or get worse, it has to have a function not only for the individual but also for the couple system. Historical factors do not automatically lead to current behaviors. One person's behavior will continue or get worse only if it confirms the partner's world view and plays a role in the larger systemic context. In the couples who come to us for therapy, the double bind is reciprocal. Each of the members is caught in a parallel paradox and neither can satisfy the other's demands.

As I suggested in the example of the therapist who associated being chosen with disaster, a similar reciprocal double bind can arise between therapist and patient. But I will show how we can take advantage of self-reference in therapy and how we can respond to both levels of our patients' double binds at the same time.

Resonance and Assemblages

I will introduce two other concepts—resonance and assemblages—that should also prove useful in our field.

Resonance occurs when the same rule or feeling appears to be present in different but related systems. Consider, for example, a family that felt they were just there in the therapist's consulting room without really being taken care of. It turned out that the therapist had experienced similar feelings in her family of origin and felt them currently in the institution where she was seeing the family and in the supervision group.

Resonances are a particular case of what I call *assemblages*. While resonances are formed of similar elements appearing in different systems, assemblages can be groupings of different elements that the therapist and the other members of the therapeutic system are able to see as connecting individual, family, social, and other themes. In the case of the family with psychotic daughters in chapter 2, we will see an assemblage in which two kinds of elements dovetail: (1) specific or intrinsic rules about keeping the mother alive and maintaining the family system, and (2) singularities peculiar to the family and therapeutic systems, notably the significance of the word *water* for the family members and for the therapist. The amplification of assemblages, composed of the intrinsic rules and the singularities of the therapeutic system, can either block change in the system or free it up.

A Journey Together

I would like to take you on a kind of journey, a journey that reflects my own professional evolution. You will learn how I passed from a view of the therapist being swallowed up by the family to one in which the therapy unfolds at the intersection of the different ways that the members of the therapeutic system construct reality. You will see how I moved from thinking of "maps of the world" held by the members of the system to thinking of their "constructions of the world" or "world views," an evolution that led me to abandon—at least for psychotherapy—the notion that the territory can be distinguished from the map.

When I first began working as a family therapist, I was

taught that families function according to the laws that govern stable open systems. Aware of the limitations of this view, I started borrowing elements from Prigogine's work on non-equilibrium systems as a way of giving therapists more freedom both conceptually and clinically. At the time, I did not question the idea of using theories from the hard sciences in the domain of human relations.

But I began to be uncomfortable with the idea of directly applying theories from sciences like thermodynamics and biology to the field of families and family therapy. I no longer feel that the same structures apply to different branches of knowledge. I want to use the work of people like Prigogine, Maturana, Varela, and von Foerster as a source of inspiration to our field. I see the relationship between their work and mine as poetic rather than scientific. (But are we so sure that poetry is outside of the realm of science?) When Varela struggles with self-reference from a mathematical point of view (in a way that is strikingly different from Whitehead and Russell's), he is useful to me not because I am trying to apply his solution to my different field but because his way of approaching the problem opens up new possibilities for me.

During the four years that I have worked on this book, I have begun to see how self-reference can be an asset for the therapist rather than a handicap. My work in couple and family therapy has been enriched by a new, and I now think fundamental, dimension. The following pages reflect the development of my own ideas. If the ideas presented are close to your constructions, then perhaps what I say here will also inspire you.

Now let us begin our journey together.

If You Love Me, Don't Love Me

1
Reciprocal Double Binds

"So, who are these flowers for?"

"For you, of course!"

"Since when do you give me flowers? What have you been up to?"

"Hey, I just wanted to give you some flowers!"

"Don't give me that! What's going on?"

"Oh, for God's sake! I can't even give you presents any more!"

"If you *really* cared, you'd have remembered that I like lilacs, instead of grabbing a few roses at the first florist you saw. Unless you just asked your secretary to get them!"

"I did not send my secretary. I picked them out myself!"

"Then how come you didn't get lilacs?"

"I forgot you liked them."

"Great! And you say you want to please me! I don't want your stupid flowers!"

The husband throws the flowers down and storms out, slamming the door.

"Thanks a lot!" his wife screams after him. "When are you going to stop torturing me?"

NOTE: Parts of the first two chapters were originally published under the following titles: "A systemic approach to couple therapy," *Family Process* 25 (1986): 35–42 and "From general laws to singularities," *Family Process* 24 (1985): 151–64.

On first reading, we might see the wife as someone who, for reasons connected to the past as much as the present, cannot let her husband give her presents, while he might be a helpless victim, caught in a difficult situation.

But on another level perhaps he participates in creating the situation he feels victimized by. We might also ask to what extent the couple's behavior is governed by interactional, rather than purely individual, patterns.

Before I present a model of reciprocal double binds that can be applied to couples and families, let us review the characteristics of a double bind (Bateson, Jackson, Haley, & Weakland, 1956/1972):

1. When the individual is involved in an intense relationship; that is, a relationship in which he feels it is vitally important that he discriminate accurately what sort of message is being communicated so that he may respond appropriately.
2. And, the individual is caught in a situation in which the other person in the relationship is expressing two orders of message and one of these denies the other.
3. And, the individual is unable to comment on the messages being expressed to correct his discrimination of what order of message to respond to, i.e., he cannot make a metacommunicative statement. (P. 208)

Jay Haley (1959) has given a good description of a reciprocal double bind:

Suppose that a mother said to her child, "Come and sit on my lap." Suppose also that she made this request in a tone of voice which indicated she wished the child would keep away from her. The child would be faced with the message, "Come near me," qualified incongruently by the message, "Get away from me." The child could not satisfy these incongruent demands by any congruent response. If he came near her, she would become uncomfortable because she had indicated by her tone of voice that he should keep away. If he kept away, she would become uncomfortable because after all she was inviting him to her. The only way the child could meet these incongruent demands would be to respond in an incongruent way; he would have to come near her and qualify that behavior with a statement that he was not coming near her. He might, for example, come toward her and sit on her lap while saying, "Oh, what a pretty button on your dress." In this way he would sit on her lap, but he would qualify this behavior with a statement that he was only coming to look at the button. Because human beings can communicate two levels of message, the child can come to his mother while simultaneously denying that he is coming to her . . . after all, it was the button he came to be near. (P. 168–69)

In the following pages I illustrate with descriptions of double binds in different contexts how this kind of communication is not necessarily contradictory but in fact responds to the internal logic of the system in which it arises. It is the price the system pays to maintain its stability, given apparently contradictory rules. In later chapters I will describe interventions that can be used in these kinds of situations.

Let me emphasize that this double-bind model, and other models I will propose later on, are only ways of organizing what I see, notions that have helped me to be freer and therefore more creative with the couples and families I have met in psychotherapy. However, they are only a springboard—if they can be useful to you, fine; if not, construct your own.

Clinical Example: Anna and Benedetto

My notions about reciprocal double binds grew out of my work with this couple many years ago. Anna and Benedetto come to consult me. She is Dutch; he is Italian. She is fed up with his suspicious behavior and accuses him of constantly following her and spying on her. She says that there is no affection between them. Benedetto says Anna is constantly cutting him off: she talks to their child in Dutch, which he doesn't understand, she is always forming alliances against him with her friends, and she is never tender with him.

I am struck by something Anna says to me after two sessions: "He has changed so much in the direction I have always wanted, and now I can't seem to deal with all this affection. I'm sad and I feel guilty about it." Benedetto's behavior seems to have had a function for Anna. As long as he was the jailer, Anna could complain about being closed in and blame him for taking away her freedom. But once he gives up this role, Anna can't face her new freedom. It's as if she has to take over his role too and become both prisoner and jailer. She is caught in a double bind; she wants her husband to stop acting in a way that forces her to reject him, but she can't accept his being close.

At another point in the therapy, Benedetto says: "I am afraid of being deserted. I am afraid of becoming attached." When Anna tries to draw closer to him, Benedetto disqualifies what she is doing by remembering a whole series of earlier approaches and thus convincing himself not to believe her. So Benedetto is also caught in a double bind. He wants his wife to be more tender, but he can't accept the closeness that tenderness involves.

How do we understand what goes on between Benedetto and Anna? Is it simply a situation where two people coexist in their separate personal worlds, or can we try to understand what happens in terms of the rules of a system which they create together and which affects them both?

When I see a couple or a family, my goal is not so much to understand what is "really" going on as it is to develop a way of looking at things that will allow them to see more possibilities in their situation. Change can arise when there are intersections between different constructions of reality. I am less interested in trying to bring out the truth as such than I am in encouraging people to look at and live their reality in more flexible and open ways. If the therapy is successful, this in no way proves that what I have said corresponds to any kind of reality. My theorizing is purely pragmatic.

Given these preliminary remarks, I will outline a model for understanding the reciprocal double binds Anna and Benedetto are caught in. They describe aspects of their life that help us form some hypotheses.

Anna talks of the extreme closeness that used to exist between her and her father; she was his favorite child. She weeps as she talks of an evening just before Christmas when she was four years old. She waited for him and he never came. He had been arrested, and her mother did not tell her. "I felt totally abandoned. I am convinced that relationships always end up like that. Friendship never lasts. Love never lasts." Benedetto adds, "Once she said to me, 'Someday you won't come back.' "

Benedetto says that he lived with his grandparents from the time he was three weeks old until he returned to his parents at the age of twelve. "It tore me up to leave my grandfather and my friends," he says. He cried every night the first year he was back with his parents. His father treated him as a "good-for-nothing" and was often brutal to him. He describes at length the coalitions he felt trapped in, not only at his parents' but at his grandparents'. A psychiatrist later told him he had a "persecution complex," but he gives examples proving to himself that he has every reason not to trust people. When he talks about how people who were close to him were snatched away, he uses the words quoted above: "I am afraid of being deserted. I am afraid of becoming attached."

I call their explicit demands the *official program*. Anna demands that Benedetto be close to her, and Benedetto demands that Anna accept him. But for each of them the official program contradicts a belief based on past experience. Anna believes that abandonment is inevitable, Benedetto, that he will be rejected. I have called this belief the *world map*.*

These maps based on past experiences govern how Anna and Benedetto perceive the present. Never mind that the world in which we live is not the same as the one we imagined when the maps were being drawn up. The system adapts itself to avoid too much disparity between the map and the territory. I am alluding here to the work of Alfred Korzybski (1953), who maintained that the map is not the territory and that an ideal map cannot exist without constant reference back to itself. The stability of a system depends on how the maps of its members influence each other and overlap.

Thus each member of the couple is torn by the contradiction between two levels of expectation (figure 1). Anna tells Benedetto, "I want you to be close." If Benedetto moves closer he follows her official program but not her world map, so she rejects his closeness. If Benedetto withdraws from her, he follows her world map but not her official program, so she complains and demands that he move closer.

Benedetto tells Anna, "I want to be accepted." If she stops excluding him, she follows his official program but not his world map, so he has to refuse the relationship. If Anna sets up new alliances against him, she follows his world map but not his official program, so he complains and demands that she accept him. We could regard this process as the way they project their internal conflicts, by living as if one level of the double bind, the world map, were imposed from the outside; but this is too simplistic.

So what do we see happening? When Anna aligns against

*Influenced by the work of Heinz von Foerster, I later abandoned the term "world map" and replaced it with "world view." I have kept the old terminology here so that the reader will be able to follow my evolution from one construction of the world to another.

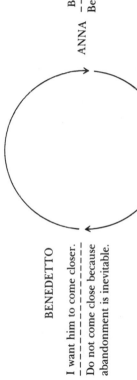

He is spying on me.
His behavior is such that
I can only reject him.

BENEDETTO

Anna's O.P.: I want him to come closer.
Anna's W.M.: Do not come close because
abandonment is inevitable.

ANNA

Benedetto's O.P.: I want recognition.
Benedetto's W.M.: I can only be rejected.

She creates coalitions with our son
and her friends against me.
I feel excluded.

O.P. = Official program
W.M. = World map

Figure 1 Benedetto and Anna's Reciprocal Double Bind

Benedetto with her son and her friends, she confirms his world map: "I'm always going to be rejected." When Benedetto spies on Anna and behaves in such a way that she has to reject him, he justifies her refusal to be close. Thus she is in no danger of finding herself in a situation where she might be abandoned.

We are beginning to see more than just two people who cannot break out of their reciprocal double bind. It is not simply a matter of their both pushing on a revolving door and blaming each other for causing the movement that makes them dizzy. They have helped each other to create a system which, governed by its own laws, imposes rigid rules and seemingly unbearable cycles of interaction on them. The function of their behaviors is to be found not just in their individual motivations but also in the context of the couple's system. What each seems to be doing to torment the other can also be described as a way of confirming the other's beliefs and helping the other avoid the risk and pain of change.

The system will expand to include the therapist as soon as one appears. The therapist will be controlled by apparently new rules which she or he helps create, but mostly the rules will maintain the therapeutic system with as little change as possible.

For example, Anna and Benedetto agree to meet somewhere before coming to a session. Benedetto doesn't show up, so Anna comes alone and asks to be seen by herself, arguing that she does not want to lose a session because of her husband. If the therapist goes along with this, he extends the rules of the couple system to the therapeutic system by forming an alliance with Anna that distances Benedetto and confirms to him the fact that he will be rejected. If the therapist refuses to see Anna alone, she may well feel abandoned and have the impression that the therapist, like Benedetto, is acting in a way that forces her to reject him.

We see a process in which Benedetto, by making a mistake

about where to meet (as I later learn), and Anna, by demanding to be seen by herself, attempt without realizing it to change the therapeutic context by applying to it the rules of their couple system.

Should we conclude from the example of Anna and Benedetto that the dynamics of a couple can be reduced to dyadic terms? I do not think so, particularly as even my hypotheses about the couple were developed in the context of the therapeutic system, in which we were three people and no longer two. But were we really three? To keep things simple, I have not insisted on the importance of their families of origin; yet as soon as we study a couple's behavior in the context of their families of origin, it becomes apparent that one of the main functions of their conflict is to maintain the rules of a system that includes these families of origin. The couple is simply the visible part of a larger system, which encompasses broader sociocultural and political elements.

Clinical Example: The Couple in Context

A young couple comes to see me. The man is a former left-wing militant. He complains that his companion never does what she wants to but rather what she thinks he expects from her. He says to her: "I want you to be free."

They are planning to leave the country in a few days and have to decide whether they will leave together. In the course of the session, the man asks the woman if she is planning to go with him. She hesitates. After a short silence, during which he becomes more and more agitated, he says, "I see you've made up your mind!" I ask him to let the young woman decide what she wants to say. New silence, new agitation, then he breaks in again: "Do you want me to step out for a moment? Do you want me to go out?" The young woman takes her head in her hands and says: "Can't we just stop for a moment? I'm completely confused."

When we look at this interaction on the first level we see a paradoxical injunction (Watzlawick, Beavin, & Jackson, 1967), which requires: (1) a strong complementary relationship; (2) within the frame of this relationship, an injunction that must be obeyed but must be disobeyed to be obeyed; and (3) the person occupying the one-down position in the relationship must be unable to step outside the frame and thus resolve the paradox by commenting on, that is metacommunicating about, it.

In this couple the paradoxical injunction is "I want you to be free," with its contradictory messages on the verbal and the nonverbal levels; this coexists with a double bind, "Be free, but I can't allow you to make a decision contrary to mine."

Are we so sure that this paradoxical injunction should be understood only in the context of the couple or of their extended families? Can we not see it in terms of the society that surrounds and molds them? In theory, people are free to make any decision they want. In fact, choices are limited, and the societal structures that constrain or restrain people's freedom are either denied or, more often, disguised under a patina of pseudobenevolence. It is not just that the couple replicate the methods of a society with which they fundamentally disagree. They may also, without realizing it, be governed by the cultural and political system and help perpetuate it in the very act of fighting it.

Clinical Example: The Therapeutic System

The therapeutic system is also susceptible to reciprocal double binds. I once consulted on the care of a family that included a father with a chronic medical problem, a mother who is a nurse, and two daughters. Fifteen years ago the mother fell and injured her knees, and then fell again. Since then she has had constant infections and operations. The family has been sent to a therapist because of the school problems of one of the daughters, but the physical problems of the family members dominate the therapy.

All the members of the family insist on how important helping is. For the mother, without helping everyone is alone; for the father, without helping no communication is possible; for the daughters, without helping there are no social relationships. Nevertheless, each time the therapist tries to help one of them, the family disqualifies her help. The therapist asks some questions to try to understand what is going on. It emerges that the father thinks a person would have to be very incompetent to ask for help; the mother says you would have to be at the end of your rope to do that; and the children both agree with their parents.

The therapist, who is one of my students, has asked me to watch this particular session over closed circuit television. I am struck by the fact that not only the mother but also both daughters come in on crutches. One daughter has a swollen knee, the other a sprain that has turned into tendonitis.

At the break in the session, the therapist and I develop the following hypothesis: this is a family where one of the important rules is to help people but where, conversely, one must never ask for help. So each member of the system is faced with a dilemma: helping is a way of participating in what unites the family, but everyone has to refuse the proferred help or break a second rule of the system.

From this point of view, physical symptoms can be seen as a way out of the contradiction. A physical or organic problem invites others to help you, but you do not have to ask them for it. Thus the family becomes a place where members offer themselves to each other as people who need help. You can eat your cake and have it too: "Help me" goes along with "I'm not asking you for anything."

When a system like this is in therapy, the members make the same demand of the therapist as they do of each other. "We are here because we need help, but we can't ask you to help us." To the extent that the therapist, in part for her own reasons, enters into this double bind, therapeutic intervention will be paralyzed. If she tries to help she will be acting as if the family can accept her help, which they cannot. If she says she is powerless or if the therapy doesn't progress, they can remind her that they are expecting results.

Moreover, if the family's rules about helping happen to overlap some of the therapist's own world maps (even if hers are not exactly the same as the family's), there may be a reciprocal double bind on the level of the therapeutic system. The therapist and family subsystems will work on each other to make sure that helping fails even while maintaining the appearance of a helping relationship.

The family just described above is a special case: the theme of helping is an explicit element in some of the family system's rules. We could argue, however, that in many instances requests for help are accompanied by implicit demands that strictly limit the therapist's ability to intervene. Whether it is an institution, a family, a couple, or an individual, the hope is often to get rid of the symptom without changing the underlying rules that have caused and are maintaining it. The therapist, or whoever else is trying to intervene, is faced with two apparently contradictory demands. This may account for the success of certain systemic therapists who tell their clients not to change. On the content level they send the message, "Don't change," but this message is denied by the therapeutic relationship, since the family is coming to them precisely in order for the symptom to change. In this way they avoid responding to only one of the two demands. The therapeutic relationship responds on one level, the overt content of the message on another.

Clinical Example: Fabienne and Chantale

Sometimes an overlap between the world maps of the protagonists in the therapeutic system leads to a temporary and precarious stability.

Fabienne, a young student beginning family therapy training, starts to tell her supervisor about a young woman named Chantale who was referred to her by a consultation service. Almost immediately the supervisor has a hard time telling whether she is talking about Chantale or about herself. Chantale left her family about ten months ago to live with a boyfriend in a smaller town; since then Fabienne and Chantale have had a weekly therapy session by telephone.

The student describes something Chantale said recently: "She told me she could no longer imagine me except as a disembodied voice, which she needed and waited for every Monday; the voice made her reflect, but it was a little like her conscience, the only difference being that I didn't give the answers she would have given."

She goes on: "I was really worried by what she said. It was flattering and touching, but suddenly I became frightened that I had created a relationship of complete dependence that seemed to me very harmful for the patient. I felt incapable of helping her get out of it."

The supervisor is struck by this unusual relationship and by the fact that Chantale has missed only two "appointments" in ten months. He learns that Chantale's mother remarried when her daughter was six years old. Chantale met her father for the first time when she was eighteen; he was an alcoholic and she decided never to see him again. In addition, serious problems developed within her family, particularly with her stepfather. Feeling completely rejected by her mother, she asked the consultation service for help. She is convinced that you cannot trust anyone—and at the same time she wants help from someone she can count on.

The parents of Fabienne, the trainee, separated when she was six. Her father, who lived abroad, had a hard time accepting the divorce and refused to see his daughters unless their mother came with them. When she was sixteen, Fabienne decided to stop seeing her father because her contacts with him had become too difficult. It wasn't until four years later, when she was living with a boyfriend, that her father got in touch with her again.

For Fabienne, autonomy is by definition painful: it occurs when someone you depend on rejects you. She wants a painless autonomy for Chantale, but doesn't think it is possible. Like Chantale, she doesn't believe other people are trustworthy enough to count on.

On the basis of this information, the supervisor constructs a working hypothesis, as diagrammed in figure 2. Chantale wants to be able to rely on Fabienne but doesn't believe this is possible: she can rely only on herself. Thus if Fabienne responds to Chantale's explicit request, she runs counter to the expectation Chantale expresses on another level. But thanks to the telephone therapy, the therapist is simply a voice that Chantale does not differentiate from herself. She is Fabienne and at the same time she is not. Chantale does not have to worry about counting on someone who may turn out to be unreliable since, after all, this other and she are one.

Fabienne wants to help Chantale achieve a painless autonomy but does not believe in it because she sees dependency as leading inevitably to rejection. If Chantale changes in the direction Fabienne overtly wants, she will run counter to what Fabienne expects on another level. But thanks to the tele-

Thanks to the telephone, for Chantale, the therapist is no more than a voice that she does not distinguish from herself. She has not been confronted with her fear of having to count on a person who might turn out to be unreliable because, after all, this person and she are one and the same.

Fabienne's O.P.:
I want a safe autonomy for Chantale.
- - - - - - - - -
Fabienne's W.M.:
Autonomy can result only from dependence followed by painful rejection.

O.P. = Official program
W.M. = World map

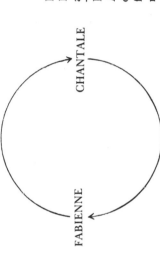

CHANTALE

FABIENNE

Chantale's O.P.:
Be reliable.
- - - - - - -
Chantale's W.M.:
One can rely only on oneself.

Thanks to the telephone, the distance gives Fabienne the illusion that Chantale is not really dependent and that therefore the risk of rejection and painful autonomy is reduced to a minimum.

Figure 2   Fabienne and Chantale's Reciprocal Double Bind

phone Chantale can satisfy both levels at once. The physical separation gives Fabienne the false impression of a certain autonomy; moreover, the distance allows her to maintain the illusion that there is not real dependency and therefore little risk of rejection and painful autonomy.

This careful balance hangs by a wire, in more than one sense. Fabienne may become frightened by the relationship which she described as "symbiotic" after their recent telephone conversation. Chantale is in danger of letting Fabienne become so important that her conviction that she can rely only on herself risks being called into question.

If the relationship is broken off, Chantale will be confirmed in her belief that she cannot trust anyone, and Fabienne will once again find that dependency leads to rejection and a forced and painful autonomy. At this point the cycle maintained and supported by the two double binds will no longer exist; but Fabienne and Chantale will have reinforced each other's constructions of reality.

Living with the Double Bind

Let me also describe a situation told to me by Jacques Pluymaekers, a friend who often deals with institutional problems. He was supervising a student teacher working in an institution for temporary care to children from troubled families. That student was having some difficulties with one of the children and wanted his help. Invited to a meal, he was intrigued by the game that was going on between the teacher and the child. The teacher kept trying to get the little girl to eat and the little girl kept stubbornly resisting. But there was an astonishing connivance between the two: the child was in fact refusing to eat when the teacher told her to—but at the end of the meal her plate was almost empty. Essentially, she was eating whenever the teacher looked away.

How can we interpret this kind of implicit collusion? The teacher acts as if a child who is eating is not eating. The child acts as if she is not eating even though she is eating. We might develop the following hypothesis: if the institution succeeds in taking better care of the children than their parents have, it acts as a rival and thus makes the families look bad. If the institution does not succeed in taking appropriate care of the children, it validates the parents but is open to criticism for failing to accomplish one of its most important functions.

Both the teacher and the little girl are caught in the parents' double demand: "Succeed but don't succeed." For its part, the institution wants to succeed, but how can it do so without disqualifying the parents? Ideally, the institution should empower the parents. If parents cannot help their children when they return from the institution, the argument for repeated placements becomes stronger and stronger. In this case, the institution will have failed in another of its goals, which is to enable children to return to their families.

By behaving as they do, the teacher and the child manage to satisfy the two contradictory levels of demand: the child who does not eat, and the teacher who complains about it, prove that the institution is not succeeding. Nevertheless, even though the teacher is right beside her, the little girl manages to feed herself, so the institution's honor is saved.

This example is another illustration of a reciprocal double bind: the institution asks the parents to succeed in order to achieve one of its goals. But if the families do succeed, the institution is either proven wrong or has to go out of business. For their part, the parents ask the institution to succeed so that their children will get better; however, if it does succeed, they have to deal with the fact that it has succeeded where they have failed, that it has "won."

The teacher and the child, caught in this "knot" (Laing,

1970) of contradictory rules, come up with an innovative behavior that is a real exercise in creative topology, enabling
them to be and not be in a place at the same time (figure 3).

Double binds are by no means rare in human systems.
David Cooper (1967) points out in *Psychiatry and Anti-Psychia-
try* that when we are confronted with a society that claims to
promote autonomy but in fact cannot accept it we are all
caught in the kind of double bind that leads to schizophrenia.
However, in some contexts the double bind can be a source
of creativity rather than pathology. Gregory Bateson (1969/
1972) underlines the creative aspect of the double bind: "It
seems that both those whose life is enriched by transcontextual gifts and those who are impoverished by transcontextual
confusions are alike in one respect: for them there is always
or often a 'double take'" (p. 272).

To support this proposition Bateson describes the actions
of a female porpoise whose trainer sets up a series of con-
fusing situations. In the course of a first experiment, the
porpoise displays a certain behavior (raising her head out of
the water, for example), hears a whistle, and then receives
food. Three successive sequences show that the porpoise has
grasped the connection between her movements and the re-
ward. During subsequent experiments, the porpoise will not
be rewarded for the same behavior: she will have to come up
with a new behavior—for example, slapping her tail on the
water—to be rewarded. Now let us imagine a third demonstration in which this new behavior, "tail slapping," is no
longer rewarded. The porpoise will end by "understanding"
what Bateson calls the "context of contexts" and will come up
with a new sequence of behaviors in each later experiment.

When we study recordings of these sequences, we see that
the trainer has to break the rules of the experiment many
times and give the porpoise reinforcements she is not entitled
to, in order to maintain his relationship with the animal. Thus,
as a result of the confusion of the rules applying to the re-

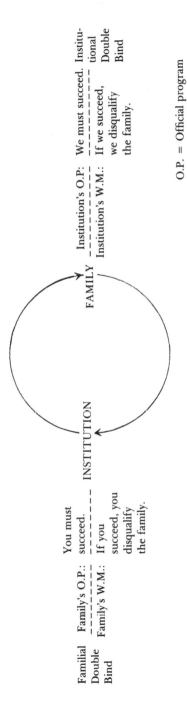

The instructor describes the child
as a non-eater when in fact she does eat.
By so doing she answers both levels
of the familial double bind.

Institution's O.P.: We must succeed. Institu-
- - - - - - - - - - - tional
Institution's W.M.: If we succeed, Double
we disqualify Bind
the family.

O.P. = Official program
W.M. = World map

FAMILY

INSTITUTION

The child behaves as if she were not
eating while in fact she is eating. By
so doing, she answers both levels
of the institutional double bind.

Familial   Family's O.P.: You must
Double   - - - - - - - - succeed.
Bind   Family's W.M.: If you
                            succeed, you
                            disqualify
                            the family.

Figure 3 The Institution–Family Reciprocal Double Bind

lationship between the trainer and the porpoise we see a change in the behavior of the trainer. This mutual "support" between the trainer and the porpoise, with its confusion of rules, in the end elicits creative acts from the porpoise, who invents new sequences of behavior.

I would like to emphasize here not only the creative aspect of the symptoms with which we are confronted, but also the central place of paradox in the human condition and the personal creativity we need to summon up, as members of a system, in order to enlarge our field of possibilities.

2
Systemic Therapy, Chance, and Change

ONE of the theoretical foundations on which the majority of family therapists seem to be in agreement is the general system theory of Ludwig von Bertalanffy (1968). Members of the Palo Alto group (Watzlawick, Beavin, & Jackson, 1967) have offered the most structured description of how this theory can be applied to family systems.

Bertalanffy tried to formulate principles valid for different sorts of systems, including, among others, biological systems and physical and chemical systems. Realizing that an attempt to apply principles from other domains to human systems would evoke a skeptical response, Watzlawick, Beavin, and Weakland (1967), citing Bertalanffy, recalled that although the law of gravitation applies to Newton's apple, the planetary system, and the tides, this does not mean that apples, planets, and the ocean are one and the same thing. Looking on interactions as systems, these authors advanced a number of formal properties valid for all open systems. Among these, the most important are totality, nonsummativity, equifinality, and homeostasis.

Totality.   Just as the change of one element of a system entails the change of the entire system, the behavior of one member of a family cannot be separated from the behavior of the other members and a change in one member's behavior changes the system as a whole.

Nonsummativity.   In the same way that a system is not merely the sum of its components, one cannot reduce a family to the sum of its individual members.

Equifinality.   In the family, as in any self-regulated system, similar outcomes can arise from differing initial conditions. If a patient presents with swollen ankles, the physician will perform tests to try to isolate the "cause" of the condition, for example, a heart condition. On the other hand, in a human system, which is an open system par excellence, it is not possible to understand the etiology of an "anorexia" or a "schizophrenia" by tracing its cause back to one initial factor or even a series of factors. This does not mean that the first years of life do not play a major role in an individual's subsequent development, but early experiences cannot be simplistically reduced to the direct causes of later behavior. We need to look at the human system within which the symptom has arisen.

Homeostasis.   Bertalanffy (1968) made only a limited place in general system theory for the concept of regulation through feedback which Cannon had already formulated in biology under the name of homeostasis. He held that "feedback systems and 'homeostatic' control are a significant but special class of self-regulating systems and phenomena of adaptation" (p. 161). Nevertheless, it is this part of general system theory that has been most widely used in systemic therapy. As early as the 1950s, Don Jackson (1957), one of the founding members of the Palo Alto school, had advanced the hypothesis that the identified patient's sickness could be construed as a homeostatic mechanism to bring back to equilibrium a family system that was in danger of changing. This fundamental perception was one to which family therapists were to attach the greatest importance. From then on, approaching a symptom became a matter of asking what function the symptom played not only on the intrapsychic level but also on the level of the broader system where the symptom had appeared and was being maintained.

Whitehead and Russell's (1925) theory of logical types has been a second major influence in our field. This recourse to the difference between logical levels is found both in Bateson's work and in the writings of many leading family therapists. Here again, it was members of the Palo Alto group who first applied the theory to the field of family therapy.

To explain what this theory is, we must examine the famous logical and mathematical paradox of the "class of all classes which are not members of themselves." In *Pragmatics of Human Communication* (1967, pp. 190–92), Watzlawick, Beavin, and Jackson note that we can divide everything in the universe into two classes—for example, the class of "cats" and the class of "noncats"—a class being the totality of all objects having a certain property. Moving one logical level higher, we can divide the universe into those classes that are members of themselves and those that are not. For instance, the class of all concepts is a member of itself because it is a concept, but the class of cats is not a member of itself because it is not a cat. Repeating the same operation, we can divide all classes into two different classes, the class of classes that are members of themselves and the class of those that are not.

It is at this point that Russell's paradox emerges. For if the class of classes that are not members of themselves is a member of itself, then it is not a member of itself, since it is the class of classes that are not members of themselves. Yet if it is not a member of itself then it is a member of itself since the fact of not being a member of itself is the property that defines membership in the class.

Watzlawick, Beavin, and Jackson point out that this is not merely a contradiction but a true antinomy, that is, a paradox arising in a formal system, because it is based on a rigorous logical deduction. To get around the paradox, they have recourse to Russell's theory of logical types. In order to reduce the paradox to a simple sophism, Russell proposes that whatever includes all the elements of a set cannot itself be a member of the set. Russell's paradox then becomes a confusion of logical types between a class and its elements whereas a class is on a higher logical level than its elements.

The members of the Palo Alto group used the theory of logical types to try to understand the pathological paradoxes of schizophrenia. They saw schizophrenics as being trapped in a field of communication where they are unable to differentiate between logical levels and where there is no possibility of choice. They even described three forms of schizophrenia—paranoid, hebephrenic, and catatonic—as possible reactions to the confusion of logical types.

It seems, however, that the use of this theory has much broader consequences for the field of systemic therapy than these authors realized. Whitehead and Russell (1925), in their *Principia Mathematica,* after describing several paradoxes including the paradox of Epimenides the Cretan, "All Cretans are liars," and Russell's paradox of the class of classes which are not members of themselves, go on to write that all of these examples have a common characteristic, which can be called *self-reference* (p. 61).

From this it follows that the theory of logical types can be interpreted as banning self-referential statements. But there is a major danger to this, as it amounts to an attempt to differentiate what is said from who says it. Richard Herbert Howe and Heinz von Foerster (1975), in their remarkable introduction to Francisco Varela's work *A Calculus for Self-reference,* demonstrate that the proposition "The properties of the observer shall not enter into the description of his observations" (p. 1) is implicit in the theory of logical types.

How is it possible for a psychotherapist to describe a reality as if she or he were not part of it? On the other hand, what value can be attributed to a discourse that is based on a reality created in the very process of mapping it? Can we accept the self-referential paradox without being reduced to confusion and powerlessness?

I have more than once criticized the application of Bertalanffy's theories to the field of systemic therapy (Elkaïm, 1980b, 1982, 1983). Fairly early on, I felt that the theories of Ilya Prigogine and his group were more appropriate to the study of human systems in the process of change, which is what systemic psychotherapists are confronted with. Other family therapists, such as Dell and Goolishian (1979) and Fivaz, Fivaz, and Kaufmann (1983), shared this same concern with change in human systems.

At the time I was attempting to apply Prigogine's theories to the field of family therapy, I realized that my inquiries were directed less to the family system as such than to the *therapeutic system,* which included both the family and myself as therapist, because I knew that I could not speak of the family system except as it revealed itself in the therapeutic context. I did not, however, grasp the full implications of this approach: I was still implicitly acting as if a map could account for the territory I was intervening in.

In this chapter I talk about a world in which instabilities can abruptly open up new possibilities. (For more on the topics introduced here, see appendix A.) In the next chapter I will discuss the paradoxical situation of therapists who talk about a world that they participate in creating by the act of describing it. In that chapter I will show how I dealt with this paradox of self-reference, without abandoning the richness of a world in which instabilities may suddenly open up new possibilities.

Systems at Equilibrium and Far from Equilibrium

Bertalanffy's general system theory has been very useful to family therapists. Nevertheless, since it applies basically to systems at or near equilibrium, it pays far more attention to how an open system remains stable within specific limits than to how it changes. A theory of systems at or near equilibrium applies to a system whose fluctuations bring it back to the same stable condition under given conditions. In a system that is far from equilibrium, however, fluctuations can, under specific conditions, be amplified to such an extent that the system evolves toward a new and qualitatively different state.

Before examining the difference between open systems at equilibrium and open systems far from equilibrium, I would like to describe certain aspects of the work of Ilya Prigogine and his group. I will offer examples from hydrodynamics and biology to present the concepts of critical values, dissipative structures, distance from equilibrium, and bifurcation.

First I am going to talk about Bénard's instability (Nicolis, 1983; Prigogine & Stengers, 1984). If we heat the lower of two plates forming the top and bottom of a vessel containing a volume of fluid, and if the temperature difference between the two plates is less than a certain threshold, the heat will rise through the fluid by conduction and will be dissipated to the outside through the upper plate. The system will remain stable and the temperature of the fluid will vary linearly from the warmer region at the bottom to the cooler one above. If we continue to heat the lower plate, we will move the system away from equilibrium; when the temperature gradient between the top and bottom plates reaches a certain *critical value,* we will see convection currents, an abrupt increase in the heat flow, and the formation in the fluid of a series of small cells (figure 4), created by the movement of the fluid rising from the lower plate, moving along the upper plate, descending,

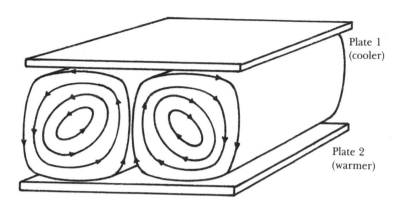

Figure 4   The motion of fluid between a warmer lower plate
(2) and cooler upper plate (1) at a threshold difference in
temperature. From G. Nicolis (1983).

moving along the lower plate, rising, and so forth. The fluid
in these cells, the *cells of Bénard,* as seen from the side, will
be moving alternately clockwise and counterclockwise
(figure 5).

Although the system's threshold of instability is determined
by environmental constraints and we can know when the
movement of the cells will appear, we cannot predict in which
direction the fluid in any given cell will rotate. The structure
formed by the cells of Bénard is called a *dissipative structure*
because it dissipates the energy being applied to the system.
It can appear only when the system is *far from equilibrium* and
requires a continuing source of energy. Once the temperature
gradient passes the critical threshold, the fluctuations no
longer tend to bring the system back to its previous state.
Instead they amplify and push the system into a new state.

My second example involves the slime mold *Dictyostelium
discoideum* (Goldbeter & Caplan, 1976). Slime molds are amoebas that live and multiply as unicellular organisms until their

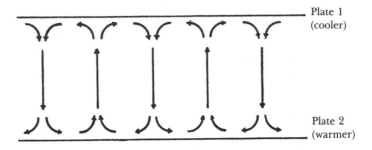

Figure 5   Movement of the cells of Bénard.
From G. Nicolis (1983).

environment can no longer furnish them with enough nu-
trients. At this point they cease to reproduce and, after a few
hours, they begin to flow together and aggregate in a wavelike
manner around cells behaving as aggregation centers. These
aggregates give rise to multicellular structures consisting of
a stalk surmounted by a fruiting head containing a mass of
spores. When the head breaks open, the spores that have
been released will produce new amoebas if the conditions are
right.

We can observe a critical value in the parameters of the
system, a point of *bifurcation* (figure 6), beyond which the
fluctuations of an attracting factor amplify by a process of
positive feedback. This amplifying factor is a chemical signal
that is sent out rhythmically by aggregation centers and is
relayed by aggregating cells. The factor attracts the surrounding amoebas, which are then incorporated into the aggregate
(Goldbeter & Segel, 1977; Susmann, 1964).

Figure 6 is a bifurcation diagram. The value K_o of a pa-

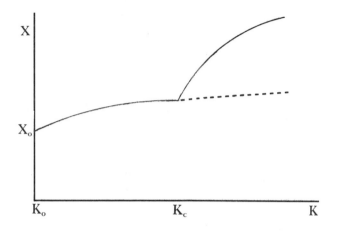

Figure 6   A diagram of bifurcation.

rameter K corresponds to the equilibrum state of the system represented by the value X_o of a variable X (X represents, for example, the concentration of a species participating in a chemical reaction). In response to an increase in parameter K, the system evolves toward a stable steady state. For a critical value K_c the steady state becomes unstable (dashed line). The new branch that appears can itself become unstable for another critical value of parameter K. This phenomenon corresponds to successive bifurcations as the distance from equilibrium increases.

Chance and Evolutionary Feedback

In addition to the four concepts just discussed, there are two others, chance and evolutionary feedback, that relate to the behavior of systems.

Chance

It is impossible to know which among many possible fluctuations will be amplified. In the case of Bénard's instability, chance alone determines whether a specific cell rotates clockwise or counterclockwise, even though strict determinism governs the moment when the cells appear.

In a similar vein, Prigogine (1977) describes Grassé's observations on the construction of termite nests. African termites begin their nests by erecting pillars; then they connect the pillars to form arches; finally they fill in the spaces between the arches. In the beginning, the termites scatter small piles of different kinds of material at random; then the smell from these materials attracts the termites to the larger piles, where the smell is strongest. Thus when a pile reaches a certain volume it attracts more termites and these deposit more material. A positive feedback mechanism enables the pillar to rise. Here again we see the amplification of a fluctuation when a certain critical threshold is passed. Below that threshold, it is not obvious that the specific small pile will become a pillar, but as soon as, by pure chance, the threshold is reached, the pillar is formed.

Gregory Bateson (1979) gives interesting emphasis to the concept of chance in his book *Mind and Nature*. He describes how when a pane of glass is struck by a stone, a pattern of radiating cracks in the shape of a star can form, but that it is impossible to predict or control the direction and position of the cracks.

The concept of chance can be very important when it is applied to family therapy. It allows us to intervene in human systems in disequilibrium without having to decide what route to follow. It is the family's own unique properties and the random amplification of certain of its singularities that will bring it to a new stage in its development. The clinical illustrations which follow will give the reader a clearer idea of how the therapist can work in situations of family disequilibrium.

Evolutionary Feedback

In certain cases a dissipative structure will cause new chemical substances to form. When this happens, the functioning of the structure may change. As Prigogine (1977) points out, the presence of these substances can lead to an increase in the rate of energy dissipation into the environment. As this occurs, the class of fluctuations that can lead to further instabilities is enlarged. He calls this process *evolutionary feedback*. These nonlinear interactions enable the system to pass through a bifurcation, a discontinuous transition, to a new state. Thus, as a result of the increase in dissipation, a dissipative structure is able to reach a new threshold of instability, which leads to a further dissipative structure, and so forth.

In an attempt to extend the concepts we have been examining to the field of family therapy, the Institute for Family and Human Systems Studies in Brussels developed, with the help of Albert Goldbeter, a member of the Prigogine group, a mathematical model describing a repetitive family interaction. Our study demonstrated that, to the extent a model can be employed, it is possible in certain specific cases to identify the points of bifurcation separating different types of behavior (Elkaïm, Goldbeter, & Goldbeter, 1980, 1987).

Stability, Instability, and History

I see two important differences in the functioning of systems in equilibrium and systems far from equilibrium.

First, in systems at or near equilibrium, stability is the rule. The behavior of the system is foreseeable because it follows general laws. In systems far from equilibrium, the evolution of the system is governed not by general laws but by properties of the system itself, for example, the nature of the interactions between its elements. These interactions can induce an unstable state and a bifurcation that abruptly separates two different modes of functioning.

Second, a system at or near equilibrium will return to its original state regardless of any perturbation to which it is subjected. The history of the system's fluctuations takes place within the norms of the system. Outside of these norms the questions of time and history are not relevant. A system far from equilibrium is capable, under the appropriate conditions, of evolving toward new modes of functioning, but the "choice" of one mode or another depends on the history of the system.

This point about history is crucial. The concept of equifinality led to minimizing the importance of history in systems. What became important, from that point of view, was to understand the present structure of the system in question. The debate that has arisen among family therapists on the place of history in human systems seems to come at least in part from the limitations imposed by Bertalanffy's approach on the role of history in systems at equilibrium. In the context of systems far from equilibrium, on the other hand, it is essential to remember the importance of irreversible processes and thus to bring back the notion of time. But reintroducing history in a systemic context does not mean reintroducing linear causality, nor does it mean giving up a view of systems that allows similar outcomes to arise from different initial conditions. Rather, it is a question of bringing back into systems a notion of evolution in time that is not reducible to terms of linear causality.

This point is important, and I will come back to it in chapters 4 and 7. At this point it is enough to say that the history of a system can be a history in which elements of the past do not automatically determine the future, owing, in part, to the chance nature of fluctuations.

Clinical Illustration: Letters and the Law

The first case involves a family of five. The parents are both professionals and about fifty-five years old. They have three children: Bertrand, twenty, Mary, seventeen, and Luke, fourteen. The family has been referred to me by the psychiatric hospital where Bertrand was a patient.

At the beginning of the first session I was so struck by the identified patient's tics that the first thing I did was ask him his name. After several attempts he managed to say "Bertrand," and at that very moment his mother told me that he had been mute for many months. I asked Bertrand not to break his silence until I could understand what it meant, and at the same time I told him that it would be hard for me to cope with letting the others speak for him. He solved this problem by communicating with me in writing.

The father described the family as having a "Christian spirit," which he said meant "obedience to the family, respect for the Ten Commandments, and faithfulness to the baptismal vows and the promises of the First Communion."

Bertrand had stopped going to school at the age of sixteen and a half. The father saw his son's problems as the result of a deep spiritual crisis. During the session Bertrand handed me a small slip of paper on which was written, "I destroy all that."

In the course of the second session, I saw that there was a strong alliance against the father among the other members of the family. Bertrand wrote, "I am Satan and the servant of Satan," but still was not able to draw the family's attention back to himself.

The morning of our third appointment, the mother called and told me the family would not be able to come in. She said her husband would send me a letter.

Here is what he wrote:

May 1

Dear Dr. Elkaïm,

I apologize for not getting in touch with you before, but I regret to inform you that we will not be keeping our appointment of May 2nd. We need some time to think things over, and we also need to be certain that both you and Bertrand's psychiatrist are expressly of the Catholic faith. I await a clear response from you on this point.

We are living at a time when, more than ever before, the Catholic faith is a "folly in the eyes of the world," including the Christian world! For the vast majority of our contemporaries, including perhaps yourself, each person has his own truth and all "truth" is subjective. Absolute Truth no longer exists.

Any true Catholic, anchored in the Faith, cannot but challenge this philosophy. If he is the head of a family, he must try to protect his wife and children against it and, if necessary, express his disapproval of behaviors which deeply violate the fundamental rules of life for all mankind, as revealed by the Creator. All of this with the understanding that such a Catholic father is always ready to forgive.

But in our Babel of a universe, the father is no longer allowed to play the role of head of his family just as there is no longer any place for forgiveness because the concept of fault, in the objective sense of the word, is rejected. This is a measure of the complete opposition that exists between Catholicism and the ideas that generally prevail today.

It is, I think, on this plane that Bertrand's case and his difficulties with his family, as well as other difficulties involving the rest of the family, lie. You will easily understand why I reject from the outset any psychiatric or psychological intervention not carried out by someone expressly asserting his attachment and fidelity to the Faith, as it has been true to itself for the twenty centuries of the Church's history. To claim to belong to a vague "Christian tradition" or to a modern Christianity that has broken with tradition is totally unacceptable to me, because either of these is likely to lead to going along with the Babel universe I have been talking about and to encourage solutions which, to the extent that they are distorted in relation to revealed Truth, can in no way be satisfactory.

Yours sincerely,

A—— A——

For me this letter had a twofold importance. The father was defending not only the values of his family and the rules that enabled it to survive, but also his vision of the world in contrast to the epistemology of the therapist, which he felt to be subversive to his own.

While respecting the father's values, I decided to borrow some elements from his letter in my reply in order to reframe positively his refusal to attend the session and to offer a paradoxical commentary.

Before I describe how I proceeded, let me pause to review the concepts of reframing and paradoxical commentary. In their book *Change,* Watzlawick, Weakland, and Fisch (1974) define *reframing* as changing "the conceptual and/or emotional setting or viewpoint in relation to which a situation is experienced and [placing] it in another frame which fits the 'facts' of the same concrete situation equally well or even better, and therefore changes its entire meaning" (p. 95). As an example of reframing they remind us of Mark Twain's Tom Sawyer. When Tom's friends start making fun of him because he is being punished by having to whitewash a fence, he convinces them that it is a privilege and has them begging him to let them do it for him.

As for *paradoxical commentary,* let us suppose that we can see the function of a certain symptom as masking contradictions or problems within the family and thus letting the system get by without changing. As long as the symptom is being described as a sickness or a behavior that comes from the patient's stubbornness, the system is "protected" by it and will not have to deal with the problems. If the therapist describes the symptom as protecting the family from these problems (which are then spelled out in detail, but with the suggestion that the patient is imagining or exaggerating them), the family system will be in a paradoxical situation. Instead of masking problems the symptom now calls attention to them; it talks out loud about things that previously could not be discussed. If it persists, it will point out what it was supposed to conceal. If it disappears, new options will develop and the therapist will be able to enter the system to open up new possibilities. Confronted with paradox, the therapist uses counterparadox (Selvini Palazzoli et al., 1978) to free the system up. I feel that the therapist's use of counterparadox is more than a strategic matter. I see the therapist as an integral part of a paradoxical situation, and if he or she makes use of counterparadox it is not in order to change levels or to escape from the paradoxical situation but rather to use it as an asset.

In this case, what I was trying to do with my reframing and paradoxical commentary was to encourage the system to stop functioning as it had been and open up new roads and broaden the range of its options. I was attempting to help the family system explore new possibilities, but I did not know what would happen next.

To use Prigogine's language, we could say that my reframing and paradoxical commentary were an attempt to disequilibrate the system by preventing it from following its old feedback loops. I was hoping in this way to amplify the fluctuations of the family system to such an extent that the system would be able to move through successive new modes of functioning by a process of evolutionary feedback. Here is what I wrote the father:

May 4

Dear Mr. A———,

I was touched by your letter of May 1st. I saw it as another demonstration of how important it is to you to protect your family in any way that you can. I don't have to remind you that, as I see it, this same concern for protecting the family is also to be found, although very differently, in Bertrand.

You wonder if psychotherapy doesn't reject the concept of fault and are afraid this means there is no longer any room for forgiveness as you understand it. And how could you fulfill your role as the head of a Christian family and continue to protect those who are dear to you without the need for forgiveness for your children and especially for Bertrand? So I understand that for you the present situation is preferable to a therapeutic outcome that could only be unsatisfactory in this larger context.

I want to convey to you my respect for your very painful choice. I would appreciate it if you would read both of our letters to your family.

With my deepest understanding,

Yours sincerely,
Mony Elkaïm, M.D.

I was trying to use this letter to change the rules of the system by reframing the illness as being preferable to the therapeutic result, suggesting that the son's illness protected, among others, the father, by allowing him to keep on forgiving, as he thought every good Christian father should. I was hoping in this way to broaden the field of what was possible for this family, without having any idea of how the family system would change. A few days later the father sent me the following letter:

May 8

Dear Dr. Elkaïm,

Thank you for your letter of May 4th. Unfortunately it does not answer the question I asked in my letter of May 1. May I briefly restate the question? As you carry out this therapy, can you respect the Revelation both in your means and in your ends; can you refrain from everything that does not respect it?

I would also like it to be perfectly clear that I do not want to "protect the faith of my family" at the expense of Bertrand's resocialization. I wish to resocialize Bertrand, but by methods that do not reject the Revelation either explicitly or implicitly, so that the members of my family can preserve the freedom to bring to the Revelation the response of their faith.

Awaiting your reply to my question, I remain,

Yours sincerely,
A—— A——

P.S. This exchange of correspondence is being shown to my family and Bertrand's family doctor.

This letter showed that the therapeutic system had gained flexibility. The father was no longer requiring that the therapist be "expressly of the Catholic faith" but simply that he respect the "Revelation."

But there was a new problem. I could not accept the father's request without becoming myself the authority on the Law of God. Leaving out the danger of taking the role of the father away from him, this could only lead to a symmetrical conflict. I therefore decided to ally myself with the family system by asking the father to continue to be the authority on the Law, both for the family and for me. In this way the implicit rules of the family could reveal themselves explicitly whenever my interventions placed them in jeopardy. In other words, I was planning to place myself on the level of the identified patient in the family system.

My position would be different from Bertrand's, however, for in fact the father would now have to name certain of the rules of the family system, while I would be in a position to comment on whatever came up. What I had in mind was a therapeutic system in which my presence could change the context out of which Bertrand's symptoms arose. To this end, I sent the following letter:

May 24

Dear Mr. A——,

Thank you for your letter of May 8th, which was waiting for me when I got back from a vacation. I respect your role too much to accept being the authority on the Law in your family. On the other hand, I am ready to work with your help if you agree to intervene every time it seems to you that I am straying from what you consider to be the path of the Law.

I would be grateful if you would read both of our letters to your family.

Yours sincerely,
Mony Elkaïm, M.D.

A month later the father sent me his answer, with a photocopy of my letter. He had underlined in yellow "being the authority on the Law" and added two question marks. He had also underlined "to intervene every time" and added an exclamation point. This confirmed for me that from now on I would be partly on the level of the identified patient to whom the father was trying to extend his law. Here is the father's letter:

June 23

Dear Dr. Elkaïm,

Thank you for your kind response of May 24th. Forgive me for being so slow to answer it.

I confess that I have not fully grasped the meaning of your letter. In addition to the natural difference in our functions, there seems to be a real philosophical divergence. If we continue with the therapy there is a danger that this uncertainty could disturb the major improvement that Bertrand has been showing for the last two months, which seems to be accelerating.

With many thanks for your work, which may have contributed to Bertrand's improvement, I remain,

Yours sincerely,

A—— A——

P.S. One more point, however. The interpretation in your last letter that I need the concept of fault in order to exercise the function of forgiveness necessary to the role of head of a family, as I am considered to conceive it—leading to my rejection of a therapy that eliminates the concept of fault—that interpretation is inaccurate. I must have expressed myself badly if I gave you that impression.

As you know, the usefulness of the Law is on the one hand to serve as a guide and on the other to enable each person to make a true judgment of himself and thus to avoid as far as is humanly possible the curse of judging others.

I myself have no *need* to forgive my son. I refuse to judge him, for judgment belongs to God. But I reject any psychiatric or philosophical discussion that disregards or denies the Law and, behind the Law, the Revelation of the Creator, who came in the form of Christ his Son to fulfill the Law and to give it its full efficacy through Grace—which is something true for all people—the sick, the healthy, psychiatrists—and for all time, as an indispensable source of the blossoming of the individual *and* of society.

I found this letter important in several respects. First, the father seemed to accept the natural difference between the therapist and himself. He thus acknowledged that I had a specific role. Second, I learned that over the two months since the correspondence had started Bertrand's condition had been undergoing continuous improvement. Third, my positive reframing of the father's rejection of therapy that did not meet his criteria and my paradoxical commentary continued to be effective. Last, the father preferred to interrupt the therapy, but without disqualifying me. In returning my letter with his annotations and in extending the Law to include me, he confirmed to me that the therapeutic system was still functioning.

I was not convinced that I would be able to achieve anything further by keeping our correspondence going. On the contrary, I feared that the father's attitude could harden, blocking any further changes in the family. So I accepted the father's request to interrupt this correspondence, not least because the exchange had allowed the therapeutic system to communicate in Bertrand's favored mode, that is, writing.

My intervention had made possible the creation of a therapeutic system with rules that were more flexible than those that governed the family system. My positive reframing of the father's behavior and my paradoxical commentary on the importance of the son's sickness were continuing to have their effect. So I sent this final letter:

July 17

Dear Mr. A——,

Thank you for your annotated copy of my letter, which you were kind enough to send me, and for your explanations and commentaries on the Law. I am particularly appreciative of the fact that you took the trouble to extend the application of the law to myself as well.

I respect your wish to interrupt the therapy in order to continue to protect the development of your family, so I am planning to end this correspondence. I would be grateful if you would read our last two letters to your family.

Yours sincerely,
Mony Elkaïm, M.D.

Clearly, what happened between the father and me was much more complex than the rationalized version presented here. I could discuss many other levels. A phrase like "the Revelation of the Creator, who came in the form of Christ his Son to fulfill the Law and to give it its full efficacy through Grace" opens up a whole range of possible comments on the relationship between the father and the son in that family. And in this particular case it is clear that something on the order of an intersection of world maps—I myself had been nurtured on readings of the Bible during my childhood and had for some years studied the commentaries of the Law— had made possible the creation of a particularly felicitous therapeutic arrangement. Further elements could be picked out, and it is precisely to the study of the interaction between different levels that the second case of this chapter is devoted.

Clinical Illustration: Singularities, Coupling, and Change

When I began to draw on the work of Ilya Prigogine for my family therapy interventions, it seemed to me it would be impossible to "recognize" the fluctuations that could be amplified to change the functioning of the system. Such fluctuations, which apparently could be amplified only by chance, seemed to fall outside of my explanatory framework. But in the case described below I discovered a theme, water, that seemed to be peculiar to the family in question and quite different from the elements that we generally use in family therapy. I call elements like this, peculiar to the individual family and not normally thought of as relevant to therapy, *singularities*. In my intervention with the family in this case, I wanted to try to amplify the singularity *water* as if it were a fluctuation that could change the way the system functioned.

Of course this singularity belonged to the therapeutic system and not just to the family system. In fact, there were two singularities that turned out to be equally important, *water* and *counting*, but for many reasons the former was more meaningful to the therapeutic system.

In this case, I not only came to appreciate more strongly

the relative importance of amplifying a singularity, but I also became aware of the crucial importance of a level to which I had paid little attention before. If we stress exclusively the search for singularity and then its amplification, we run the risk of going back to an interpretative approach, acting as if our therapeutic task is to uncover and amplify a particularly meaningful element. What I realized in studying this case, and others, was the importance of the level I call *assemblages* of singularities, in which I include the nonverbal behaviors of the members of the therapeutic system, their tones of voice, cultural references, and the like.

This level is also outside of the explanatory frameworks normally used in family therapy. Whether or not the therapist uses a structural approach, or emphasizes the meaning or function of the symptom, the level of assemblages is always present. It is very close to what Félix Guattari (1979 and 1988) calls the *semiotic level* in contrast to the level of *intrinsic rules,* that is, rules that are peculiar to the system and govern it. In my opinion, the fluctuation that is amplified is made up not of one singularity but of several, and these singularities involve both the therapist and the family. The concept of assemblages helps us understand whether a system changes or stays the same. Whatever the theoretical framework of the therapist, it is the amplification or nonamplification of the assemblages of singularities created by the therapeutic system that determines whether the system will change.

I will illustrate what I mean with a case in which I worked both on the level of the system's intrinsic rules and on the level of its singularities. The case involved a North-African Jewish family with three psychotically disturbed daughters. The father had been dead for many years. I saw the family as a consultant at the request of two of my students, who were treating the daughters. The session I quote from below was the first of two in which I took part.

The session was attended by the mother, the eldest son,

Albert, who was about thirty, and two of the daughters, Rachel and Susan, twenty-six and twenty-two, respectively.

I asked the mother about herself. She answered: "With me it's like the sea. It comes and goes. . . . It casts me on one side and then casts me back on the other. It sways me to one side and then sways me back to the other."

When I asked her to tell me more about herself, she said: "I . . . they talk about themselves. Better them than me. For me it's nothing. I'm old now. I don't count any more. I'm only waiting for the hot water."

Mony Elkaïm: What is the hot water?

Mother: Well, it's to wash me with.

M.E.: How old are you?

Mother [*To Albert*]: How old am I? I'll soon be sixty, right, Albert?

Albert: That's right. Yes.

Mother: How old?

Albert: Yes, yes, sixty.

Mother: They're the ones that count. Me, I don't count.

M.E.: And at sixty you're already thinking of the hot water? What hot water?

Mother: Yes, that's how life is.

I realized that she was referring to the hot water they use to wash the dead in North Africa. Later, when I asked her what she would do if her daughters and son got married, she replied: "I don't know what I'm going to do. Look after children. I'm going to work in a bath house, a Turkish bath. I love water. I love water. I love it very much, water."

This talk helped me form a hypothesis about the function of the symptoms of the three daughters, whose psychiatric problems had appeared just at the point when they were beginning to think about leaving home. The symptoms could be understood as a way of preserving the family's equilibrium, which was endangered by the daughters' age: if they didn't get sick, one by one they would leave the family, and this could create a new and dramatic situation as shown by the mother's remark about the hot water.

But in addition to this classical systemic reading of the situation, I was faced with the family singularity around the theme of water, a theme that was also reflected in Rachel and Albert's actual first names, which were biblical names directly evocative of water. I decided to amplify the singularity *water* without restricting it by any kind of interpretation.

Susan spoke of water as her element, as a caress, and then went on to talk of her relationship with her father and her conflicts with her mother. When I asked Rachel to talk about water, she replied, "It's as if . . . I have to speak about water as if it were . . . everyone works with their own matter."

M.E.: And what is your matter?
RACHEL: That's just it. I've evaporated and I haven't found any matter.
M.E.: Well, tell me about this state of evaporation.

Rachel burst into tears and Susan joined her. The brother started sweating. I moved over to a seat beside Rachel, and I began to sweat too. The mother was crying and handing out tissues to everyone. Then she told Rachel: "Don't cry. *Nkoun kpara.** Everything will be all right."

Three minutes went by while the mother and the two

Nkoun kpara is a Judeo-Arabic phrase meaning "Let me be your kapara." A *kapara* is an animal, generally a chicken, that North African Jews sacrifice on the eve of Yom Kippur to atone for their sins.

daughters wept and the therapists and the son sweated and no one said anything. Then Rachel told me, "I feel better." I got up and returned to my place. "Good," I declared, then added with a sigh: "I have to say something, Rachel. When I was sitting next to you I felt an extraordinary peace. I haven't felt like that for a long time. I was so serene. It's strange. It's as if your tears help the people around you to feel more connected with themselves, calmer. It's funny. Normally when you're next to someone who's crying, you don't feel right. You don't feel at ease, you feel. . . . But when I was sitting next to you . . . it was as if you made me able to just allow time to pass. It didn't matter any more." This intervention positively connoted Rachel's symptom even as it underlined the way it froze time at a specific stage in the family's life cycle.

M.E.: Don't you have the impression that in your family when someone is having a difficult time you all feel calmer?
MOTHER: Yes, yes.
M.E.: What happens? Tell me how that happens.
MOTHER: Even though we have big fights and all that, we . . . we're peaceful. There's something that . . . that unites us.

Then I pointed out to Rachel that she had kept her coat on even though she seemed to be hot. She replied that taking off her coat was like unveiling herself.

M.E. [*Turning to Albert*]: Albert, what does water mean to you?
ALBERT: The sea . . . it's an important element, because we lived by the sea. . . . It's a natural element, like fire.
M.E.: What is fire?
RACHEL: [*At the same time as Albert*]: It isn't a natural element.
ALBERT: The sun.
RACHEL: It's man who needs fire.

M.E.: What do you mean by that?

RACHEL: No, because when you need fire you have to create it, you have to create the flame. But the sea, you find it or you don't; you don't look for it. For fire, you have to look for little flints. You create the flame and man needs it. You need fire. There's the sun, of course. It warms us, but it warms too big a surface. You need a little flame.

M.E.: Would you have liked a little flame?

RACHEL: A little flame, yes.

M.E.: Not a big flame?

RACHEL: Wanted: a little flame.

M.E.: That sounds like an ad in the personal section of [the French newspaper] *Libération.* "Wanted: a little flame."

RACHEL: No, no. It's not an ad in the paper.

M.E.: Big flames can evaporate you; they can. Little flames, they respect you.

RACHEL: That's it! Little flames.

At that moment, Albert began talking about water again and we both realized the connection between water and his real first name in Hebrew.

SUSAN [*smiling*]: That's beautiful.

M.E.: I feel like a break. It's like being in a bath, where you feel good but you also feel a little tired. So I'm going to the other room to rest a little, to talk to my colleagues, and then I'll be back.

When I got back a few moments later, the mother had put on her coat and Rachel had taken hers off. After commenting briefly on that, I continued:

M.E.: I'm going to tell you what we've been doing in the other room. The first thing that struck me when I went back there was how moved they were. We all felt the extraordinary warmth you project, and how close you are to each other. When Rachel cries, Susan cries and Albert sweats and even I start sweating. [*To the mother*] And you, you cry and get out your tissues. And we all said: "How fascinating! Here's a family that fate has not been gentle to . . . and it's as if you had all gotten together again, like that."

MOTHER: Yes.

M.E.: To hold together somehow.

MOTHER: I was doing good things so that I could keep my . . . so I could solid my . . . how do you say solid, when you make something solid? . . . I consolidate the person, and I don't know if . . . it flew away as if someone had torn something away from me, had taken that tree branch, had torn it away.

M.E.: What were you consolidating? What person?

MOTHER: My family.

M.E.: We felt that too. That this family was a person. About the great difficulty, for example . . .

MOTHER [*Interrupting*]: We didn't feel that anything at all was bad.

M.E.: Yes.

MOTHER: Nothing bad. I always said: "It doesn't matter. It will blow over. Everything." But not tearing something away like that.

M.E.: At one point you said a word, you said something in Arabic to Rachel. What was it?

MOTHER: *Nkoun kpara.*

M.E.: I'm struck by the fact that a mother says, "*Nkoun kpara,* let me be your *kapara.*" I have the impression that in this family everyone is the *kapara* for everyone else. It's as if each of you were diving in—since we are talking about water—to be the first to take all the bad on himself so that the others can breathe. So what have we got? We have a mother who says, "For me, nothing matters as long as they are happy." We have Susan who, even though she is saying, "I want to be out of here," cries as soon as Rachel cries. We have Rachel, who has been a perpetual *kapara* for years. And then there is Albert. Albert works, he brings home money, he looks after his sisters, he makes sure everything holds together: that's his way of sacrificing himself too.

MOTHER: Yes.

M.E.: When I see you all like that, I say to myself, "Here's a family of people who have suffered a great deal and who, each in their own way, try to sacrifice themselves so that the others can breathe."

MOTHER: Yes.

M.E.: And I say to myself that for the time being it's too early to begin anything, because, first of all, I have to respect the way you have managed, as you say, to preserve the family.

MOTHER: Yes . . . to consolidate.

M.E.: Right. So for the time being all I want to do is to speak to your sufferings, Rachel, to your difficulties, Susan, to the burden that you [*indicating the mother*] are carrying, and that you are carrying too, Albert. What I mean is that each of you in your own way has been trying to be the savior of the family. But how can anyone save their own family? You need distance from the family to do the kind of work that, for example, we do. We try to help people, but we have to keep a certain distance in order not to be swallowed up in the process.

MOTHER: Yes, that's true.

M.E.: I think what weighs on you a great deal is the fact that you are so close to each other. . . . Like when one of you [*indicating Susan*] puts her fingers in her mouth, her sister starts biting her nails at the same time. As if the family were one "person," as you say.

MOTHER: Yes, I think you're right.

M.E.: You said, "Let me be your *kapara*," to your daughter Rachel, but you all try to be *kaparas*. I'm wondering how we can help you keep on loving each other without having to be *kaparas* for each other. At the end of Yom Kippur, the kids carry the *kapara* to the synagogue, eating one of its wings or a drumstick. Can we end up like that?

During this session I worked on two levels. In the first place, as I was amplifying the singularity *water*, I set in motion a whole series of elements on the level of assemblages of singularities—the connection of the therapist and the family around a common culture, the relationship with the Bible, the specific ways the therapist and the family members expressed themselves, my changing places to sit silently by Rachel the way North Africans do when mourning, the family's tears and my own sweating, and so forth. These elements can be seen as having a meaning and a function in the context of our usual explanatory frameworks, but they can likewise be looked on as assemblages of singularities with a meaningful existence outside our normal way of understanding things. Thus the theme of *water* can be seen as a metaphor with a meaning, and at the same time it can have a life of its own.

In this example, it is possible that things like my sweating, the family members' tears, nonverbal behaviors, and the layout of the room had a meaning and a function, but they can also be seen as an assemblage of singularities capable of keeping the system stuck or bringing about qualitative change.

I was not trying to interpret or create insight, but rather, in the language of far-from-equilibrium thermodynamics, to enter the system in order to move it away from equilibrium and allow fluctuations to be amplified until, by bifurcation or otherwise, the system's functioning changed. I behaved as if assemblages of several coupled elements could be considered as fluctuations to be amplified. These assemblages were not limited to genetic, biological, or other purely individual elements. They also involved other elements connected with but not reducible to the individual, such as the mass media, culture, and the society at large.

I also wanted to positively reframe the symptoms of the two daughters who were present at the session without separating them from the rest of the family. I hoped to create a situation that changed the way the system evolved because from now on when someone behaved in a symptomatic way she would be seen not as sick but as sacrificing herself for the family, which would lead to a different reaction. I also tried to create a therapeutic framework in which the therapists could occupy a new place while remaining allied with the family.

The therapists and I agreed that I would see the family one more time. Five weeks later the family returned. A second son, who was still a student, also came. Rachel was well dressed and well made up. She no longer looked lost the way she had in the previous session. The mother said: "The little one is better, thanks to God. If only things can continue this way. I thank God that she no longer screams the way she used to."

Systems and Assemblages

I would like to stress the importance of assemblages of singularities, which are connected to the therapeutic system. It is the development of these assemblages that determines whether the system changes or not. Will they be amplified? Will they modify the rules that govern how the system evolves?

From this point of view it is neither the individual nor a system made up of interacting individuals that is crucial, but rather developing assemblages formed of the most diverse elements. These elements cannot be reduced to obvious components of the system in question nor, certainly, to biologically determined individuals.

This point ties directly to the position of Félix Guattari (Elkaïm et al., 1982, reprinted here as appendix A): "The concept of individual unity strikes me as misleading. To claim on the basis of such a unity to be able to center a system of interactions between behaviors arising in fact out of heterogenous components that cannot unequivocally be located in one person appears to me to be an illusion" (p. 60).

In some ways this position also relates to what Bateson (1970/1972) says about the futility of trying to draw a boundary around an individual's mental system. He cites the examples of a woodcutter felling a tree or a blind man exploring his surroundings with his cane and insists on the importance of studying the total information circuit. Varela (1979) raises a similar question when he reminds us that "the knower is not the biological individual" and notes that "the autonomy of the biological and social system we are in goes *beyond* our skull" (p. 276).

In moving from a vision of a world centered on the individual to a systemic vision, we have taken a major qualitative step, but don't we still to a considerable extent look at human systems as systems of individuals in interaction? My intent is not to replace units called individuals with other units but rather to concern myself with interconnections, or, as Guattarri (1979) would say, arrangements of elements of many sorts that can vary from one moment to the next.

The notion of assemblages could turn out to be particularly useful in this context, since assemblages are made up of genetic, biological, and historical elements as well as cultural and social aspects. Composed of the most diverse elements, these assemblages would be what we are made of, without being reducible to ourselves; and it would be thanks to the intersections of these assemblages that what we call "human systems" would be formed—systems that depend more on the intersection of different assemblages than on individuals in interaction.

The kind of analysis I am talking about is complex, but I do not think that this is an insurmountable obstacle to the approach. It allows us to continue to study the systems we are part of without being limited to the overly restrictive notions of meaning or function.

3
Self-Reference and Family Therapy: From Maps to Maps

Objectivity and the Self-Referential Paradox

As a general rule, an observer who wants to study a system is required to propose hypotheses about how the system works and then to test them in order to create the best possible map of the territory being explored. It has traditionally been considered that the observer should place herself or himself outside of the system to maintain "objectivity"; failing this, the observer may contaminate the description of what is being observed. This approach, then, insists that mapmakers must exclude themselves from their maps so as not to be engulfed in a self-referential paradox.

Let us go back to the statement "I am lying": if I am telling the truth I am lying, but if I am lying I am telling the truth. As Heinz von Foerster (1984a) points out in criticizing the concept of objectivity just described, a science that needs solid foundations can deal with what is true or false but has a hard time coping with paradox. By a sort of tacit agreement, we act as if there really were a world outside of ourselves whose outlines we can quietly describe, a territory that we can calmly map.

The following example will show clearly that this objectivist position is untenable when it comes to both psychotherapy and supervision. The event took place at a workshop in an

international congress on couple therapy that I had organized. One of the therapists in the workshop described a
couple that was stuck in a repetitive cycle: the wife complained
of being constantly "invaded" by her mate, as she had been
by her parents. The husband said he was having trouble putting up with the relationship.

As I listened to the therapist's presentation, I found that
her way of expressing herself led me more and more to try
to get her to clarify what she was saying. It seemed to me that
each time I interrupted her, she encouraged me by nonverbal
signs—essentially by moving closer to me—to continue my
interruptions. So I was amplifying this process until she an-
nounced that it was the act of talking that was important to
her, not what she actually said. I realized then that we had
gotten caught in a vicious circle: my questions kept the therapist from expressing herself more clearly, while she, by expressing herself unclearly and moving closer during my
interruptions, invited me to continue "invading" her. The
intersection between the functioning of the patient couple
and the therapist/supervisor system began to become clear in
this invasion of the woman by the man.

Then the therapist told me that another man had given
the wife a bottle of perfume. The husband, she said, had
found out and thrown it away. I asked if the wife had hidden
the present from her husband, and the therapist said no. A
few moments later, though, she took it back and said the wife
had hidden the bottle of perfume and the husband had
found it only some months later when he was going through
her drawers. She went on to say that she had hidden this
from me because I kept interrupting her. Again, the functioning of the two dyads, husband/wife and therapist/
supervisor, showed an intersection. The therapist hid things
from her supervisor as the wife did from her husband, while
the supervisor for his part set up a context that favored her
doing so.

It is rare that supervision lets us see such an extreme example, showing so clearly that what we observe cannot be separated from what we feel. But in varying degrees our perception of what is happening in the systems we are part of can never be separated from the different assemblages of behaviors and ideas in which we and the other members of the system are involved. Our own construction of reality depends on the intersection of these assemblages. (I will discuss the concept of assemblages further in chapter 6.)

The self-referential aspect inherent in situations similar to the one described above led me to an interest in the works of the Chilean biologists Humberto Maturana and Francisco Varela and of the Austrian-born American cybernetician Heinz von Foerster.

From Color Vision to the Closed Nervous System

When Lettvin, Maturana, McCulloch, and Pitts (1959) published their seminal paper, "What the Frog's Eye Tells the Frog's Brain," they never questioned the existence of an objective reality independent of the animal. In 1961, Maturana and his colleague Samy Frenk began their study of the vision of pigeons with the same belief. It was only in 1964 that Maturana and Samy Frenk, joined by Gabriela Uribe (Maturana, Uribe, & Frenk, 1968), ran into problems with this assumption. The three were unable to correlate the activity of the retina with physical stimuli external to the organism, finding that under certain conditions their subjects reacted to the colors of specific objects in ways that bore no relationship to the wavelengths of the light coming from the objects.

Von Foerster (personal communication) has described the

significance of this finding. To understand Maturana's ideas of color vision, he says it is

important to distinguish between the phenomenology of the physics of electro-magnetic radiation and that of our experience of colors.

The nature of electro-magnetic radiation, ranging from X-rays to radio waves, including the range of visible light, is well understood. . . . The distinction between wavelengths in [the visible range of] the electro-magnetic spectrum and our perception of various hues is blurred when—as in classical experiments—white light (by going through a prism) is split into its spectral components whose wavelength is measured at different spots that we perceive as having different hues (from red to orange to yellow, etc., to purplish blue), and the conclusion is made that the colors so perceived are in a one-to-one relation to the corresponding wavelengths of the electro-magnetic radiation. When combinations of these wavelengths occur, the observation that there are three types of . . . retinal receptor cells that are sensitive to three different regions of the spectrum allows [us] again, by a superposition of the relative activity of these cells, to account for an apparent one-to-one correspondence between experience and radiation.

However [Goethe and many others] demonstrated that the experience of color at some point in the visual field that is illuminated with an invariable spectral distribution may change dramatically when the surrounding spectral conditions are changed. In other words, the experience of color is a global, not a local, phenomenon.

This insight creates an insurmountable problem for experimental physiologists who wish to establish "objectively" the relations between stimuli and sensations, for they cannot monitor with micro-pipettes the global activity of the retina, only the responses of single neurons, or bundles of neighboring fibers, to external stimuli.

The only one who can reliably report what she or he sees at a given spot is, of course, the experiencing subject. However, we could never know what this subject experiences unless this experience can be related through language to others, that is, "objectified." This is where Maturana comes in with his notion of colors emerging in the linguistic domain.

Deciding to explore the relationship between retinal activity and the subjective experience of colors, Maturana and his colleagues found that it was possible to establish correlations between naming a color and states of the subject's neuronal activity rather than between naming the color and the wavelength of the stimulus (Maturana & Varela, 1980; see also Maturana & Varela, 1987, and Varela, 1984). These states were determined not by the characteristics of the perturbing agent but by the individual structure of each person. This finding led them to conceive of the nervous system as a closed circuit whose activity is determined by the system itself, with the exterior world serving only as a trigger for the activity of a system whose activity is governed by its internal organization.

The results of this study, which allowed them to demonstrate how the observer's experience of color is generated, were published in an article (Maturana et al., 1968) whose impact was relatively limited at the time. Its authors emphasized that while we implicitly assume that all situations in which we experience a given color have one invariable element, this element may not belong to the world that is outside of us. It could be created by the relationship between the eye and the environment and would therefore not be "independent of the anatomical and functional organization of our retina" (p. 1).

These researchers' fundamental contribution was to establish that in order to understand the functioning of the nervous system we must see it as a closed system and "treat the report of the color experience as if it represented the state of the nervous system *as a whole*" (Maturana & Varela, 1980,

p. xv, emphasis added). As soon as one considers the nervous system to be a closed network of interacting neurons, perception is no longer a process of apprehending external reality but rather an act of specifying what reality is, and any distinction between perception and illusion becomes impossible to make. These conclusions led Maturana at a later date to consider the problems of knowledge from a biological point of view.

The Exterior World and the Structure of the Nervous System

Francisco Varela (1984) also uses an example from color vision to criticize the notion that the experience of color must be associated with the properties of the object. He describes the following experiment, which was first performed by Otto von Guericke in 1672.

Imagine two projectors arranged as in figure 7, one with a red filter and one without a filter. If we put our hand in front of the projector without the filter, we will see, as we would expect, the shadow of our hand in red against a pink background. All we have done is block the white light of the projector without the filter.

Now let us put our hand in front of the projector with the red filter. Although we might expect to see a whitish shadow against a pink background, in fact the shadow we see is bluegreen. But if we check the actual wavelengths of the light with a spectrometer the shadow turns out to be white.

Another particularly enlightening example is cited by Maturana (Maturana & Varela, 1980) in his introduction to *Autopoiesis and Cognition*. In the early 1940s Stone (Maturana & Varela, 1980, p. xv; see also Maturana, 1983, p. 256, and Maturana & Varela, 1987, pp. 125–26) surgically rotated the

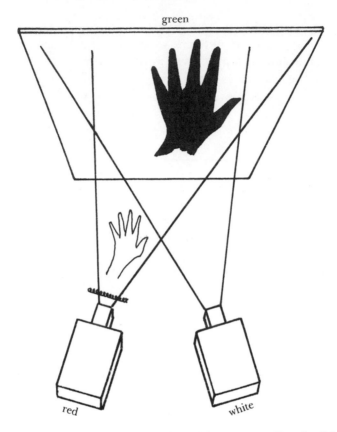

Figure 7   Experiment in color vision. From Varela (1984).

eyes of salamanders and frogs. In one experiment, he rotated one eye of a tadpole 180 degrees. When the tadpole had become a frog, if he covered the altered eye the frog would dart its tongue at its prey with perfect accuracy, but if he uncovered the altered eye and covered the good one, the frog would dart its tongue 180 degrees in the wrong direction.

The operation created a rotation in the frog's world. We observe that for the frog there is no up or down, no front or back, outside itself. What counts is the internal correlation between the part of the retina that receives the perturbation of the light waves and the movement of its tongue.

The field of visual perception allowed Maturana and Varela to call into question the view of perception as nothing but an operation limited to sending messages along "an incoming telephone line" (Maturana & Varela, 1987, p. 163) to the brain. Varela (1984), for example, has noted that for every nerve fiber reaching the cortex from the retina by way of the lateral geniculate nucleus there are a hundred others originating in different parts of the cortex and subcortex. In addition, that same lateral geniculate nucleus, which has been called the switching station of the cortex, receives at least five nerve fibers from different parts of the cortex for every one from the retina—including nerve fibers feeding back from the visual cortex (Maturana & Varela, 1987). This means that the lateral geniculate nucleus depends not only on the activity of the retina but also on the mutual relationship between connections emanating from different parts of the brain.

But a problem arises. If we abandon the notion that the nervous system collects information from the environment in order to form representations of the world, without which we could not react to it, how do we avoid falling into the solipsism of a universe where the only reality is an internal one?

Maturana and Varela (Maturana & Varela, 1987; Varela, 1984) propose to navigate between the Scylla of representationalism and the Charybdis of solipsism by inviting us to consider the organism both as a system endowed with its own internal logic and as a unity in complex interaction with the external world. Varela (1984) offers a pragmatic response to the dilemma. Perception, he says, cannot exist without an interaction between the organism and visible light waves. But the process triggered by light waves when they perturb the organism's visual receptor cells is open to many possibilities. For each organism it is the structure of the nervous system, and consequently the history of the organism that has led to this structure, that determines what happens. Color discrimination cannot exist without interaction; nevertheless, color does not reside in the wavelengths of the light.

In processes like vision, what is important is not only the perturbations acting *on* the nervous system but also the manner in which the nervous system reacts to these perturbations. Its structure changes itself to accommodate to these changes while maintaining its integrity within the environment. Faced with perturbations, the nervous system maintains certain unchanging relationships between its components, whether these perturbations are created by its internal dynamic or by its interactions with the environment.

Communication and Language

Communication, as Maturana and Varela (1987) use the word, is not the transmission of information. Communication for them is a coordination of behaviors in a domain made up of structural couplings (see appendix B). There is no information independent of the structures of the person who is speaking and the person who is listening. Information does not exist in and of itself: the information received is located at the intersection of the receiver and the transmitter. We see this in an article by Adam Rayski and Stéphane Courtois (1987) that appeared in the Paris newspaper *Le Monde*. Trying to explain why well-informed people could have doubted the existence of the Nazi extermination camps in 1943, they quote the well-known French journalist Raymond Aron, who was in London at the time: "The gas chambers, the industrial assassination of human beings, I must admit that I couldn't imagine them and since I couldn't imagine them, I didn't know they existed."

Human beings, according to Maturana and Varela (1987), cannot be freed from the web of structural couplings that language weaves. In their opinion, language was not created by the individual in order to grasp the external world. We are *in* language, situated in a linguistic structural coupling within which we construct and perfect ourselves.

The Emergence of the Observer

Maturana (1990) maintains that determinism and prediction are two totally distinct phenomena. The predictability of a system is not inherent in the system; it is linked to the relationship existing between the system and the predicting observer. Similarly, von Foerster (1984a) emphasizes that properties that are assumed to reside in things turn out in fact to be connected to the observer. Thus both inevitability and randomness reflect our own power or lack of it, not nature's.

Varela (1975) for his part stresses the role of the observer. The observer describes the world by making distinctions, but these descriptions are self-referential or reflexive:

The distinctions made which engender our world reveal precisely that: the distinctions we make—and these distinctions pertain more to a revelation of where the observer stands than to an intrinsic constitution of the world which appears. . . . In contrast with what is commonly assumed, a description, when carefully inspected, reveals the properties of the observer. We, observers, distinguish ourselves precisely by distinguishing what we apparently are not, the world. (P. 22)

Varela (1988), while bearing in mind von Foerster's insistence on the importance of including the observer in the description, distinguishes between von Foerster's imperative form of reflexivity and what he calls engendered reflexivity. In his eyes the basic problem is not so much including the observer as showing how the observer emerges in the act of observation. If you talk of "including" the observer you run the risk of suggesting that there is an entity called "the observer" independent of the system being observed. For Varela, on the other hand, we emerge as observers in the context of human behaviors and interactions, both verbal and nonverbal, in a specific time and place.

Paradox and Autonomy

Varela (1975) also offers us a way to confront Whitehead and Russell's (1925) implicit ban on self-reference in the theory of logical types. After pointing out that self-referential situations—for example the brain thinking about itself and the observer being the observation—are ubiquitous, he notes that the difficulties of dealing with self-reference are rooted in language. Paradox can appear when language deals with itself. The difficulty with self-reference arises because the distinction between actor and what is acted collapses.

There seems to be an irreducible duality between the act of expression and the content to which this act addresses itself; self-referential occurrences blend these two immiscible components of our cognitive behavior and engender a dual nature which, apparently, succeeds in escaping this universal behavior and thus seems peculiar in our knowledge. Their peculiarity lies . . . in standing out of a background by their own means, in being *autonomous.* (P. 5)

In the same article, "A Calculus for Self-reference," Varela provides us with a mathematical foundation for the existence of a distinct domain, the self-referential autonomous state. Therefore, instead of trying to avoid self-reference we can let it appear freely by taking its "apparent anomaly as a characteristic, namely, autonomy, which we find in so many of our descriptions that it seems futile to avoid rather than confront it" (p. 21).

Act Always so as to Increase the Number of Choices

Von Foerster (1984b) suggests the following experiment: hold this book in your right hand, close your left eye, and fix your right eye on the star in figure 8. Now move the book back and forth along your line of vision while keeping your eye focused on the star until at an appropriate distance (about twelve to fourteen inches) the round spot on the right disappears. If you keep the book at this distance and your eye on the star, the spot should remain invisible even if you move the book to the right, to the left, up, or down. This localized blindness arises from the absence of receptor cells on the blind spot of the retina where the optic nerve begins.

Von Foerster stresses that we do not experience a dark area in the part of our visual field where the spot should be. That would mean that we were seeing. *We are not aware of our*

Figure 8   Experiment in localized blindness.
From von Foerster (1984b).

localized blindness. This experiment is interesting not because it shows us we don't see but because it shows us we don't see that we don't see, as von Foerster is fond of saying. He calls this a second-degree problem and says that when it comes to visual perception we should change the saying "Seeing is believing" to "Believing is seeing."

Von Foerster (1984b) raises a point to which Maturana and Varela also attach a great deal of importance. Noting that our nervous systems have a hundred million sensory receptors and ten trillion synapses, he concludes that "we are 100,000 times more receptive to changes in our internal than in our external environment" (1984b, p. 52). He uses the word *computing* to describe any operation that transforms, modifies, arranges, or rearranges physical entities or symbols. For von Foerster (1984a), *autopoiesis* (discussed in appendix B) is organization that computes its own organization and autopoietic systems are systems that are thermodynamically open but organizationally closed.

Von Foerster (1984c) distinguishes between trivial and nontrivial machines. The basic difference between the two is that in a nontrivial machine a specific stimulus can lead to more than one response. "Obedience is the hallmark of the trivial machine; it seems that disobedience is that of the nontrivial machine. However . . . the non-trivial machine is obedient, but to a different voice. Perhaps one could say it is obedient to its inner voice" (p. 10). A hand calculator is a trivial machine; a car is a nontrivial machine. Von Foerster points out that if our car doesn't start when we turn the key we try to suppress its unpredictability by taking it to a mechanic, a specialist in retrivialization. But in human affairs, trivialization leads to a limitation in the available choices. Von Foerster (1984b) argues instead for detrivialization, or, as he had put it earlier, the ethical imperative: "Act always so as to increase the number of choices" (1984b, p. 60).

Autonomy and Ethics

Von Foerster postulates that "the nervous system is organized (or organizes itself) so that it computes a stable reality," and this self-regulation of the living organism is for him a synonym for autonomy, that is, regulation of regulation (1984b, p. 58).

But autonomy does not necessarily lead to solipsism. Von Foerster encourages us to imagine a little man in a bowler hat who takes the classical solipsist position that he is the only reality and that everything else exists only in his imagination. But he cannot deny that his imaginary universe is peopled with apparitions like himself and that they too may claim to be the only reality, with everything else existing only in their imaginations.

According to what von Foerster refers to as the *principle of relativity*, we must reject a hypothesis when it does not hold for two instances together, even if it holds for each of them taken separately. For example, Earthlings and Venusians may both claim to be the center of the universe, but their claims will break down if they ever get together. Under the principle of relativity, "the solipsistic claim falls to pieces when I invent another autonomous organism" (1984b, p. 59). Of course the principle of relativity is not a logical necessity, nor can it be proved or disproved. I am free to reject it or accept it. If I reject it I am indeed the center of my universe; but if I accept it, neither I nor anyone else can be the center of the universe. There has to be a point of reference that connects us both. This is identity, the relation between Thou and I. If I accept the principle of relativity, Reality equals Community. This is a profoundly ethical position. Autonomy, as Kant pointed out (Howe & von Foerster, 1975), is central to responsibility, and without responsibility there can be no ethics.

Self-reference and Family Therapy

What relevance do these theories have for family therapy? In the early years of the family therapy movement, the approach was rich in clinical tools but limited in its theoretical underpinnings. The work of the Palo Alto group on the relationship between general system theory and family systems led to the gradual emergence of a dominant theoretical approach. Based as it was on isomorphisms between systems, it tried to extend general laws valid for different open systems to family systems.

The work that some of us did on the basis of the research of Prigogine and his team was still conducted from this perspective. We tried to create more freedom in the field of systemic therapy by drawing on the domain of systems far from equilibrium. It was in this way that we developed, one after the other, the importance of rules specific to the individual family, the effect of apparently trivial fluctuations that are capable of being amplified, the role of chance, and the place of history in a world that is not governed by linear cause and effect. We also realized that the processes we were examining took place in the therapeutic system and not just in the family system. But how could we talk about a therapeutic system in which we were participants? How could we intervene? These are the questions that led us to the work of researchers who were studying self-reference.

But I was no longer concerned with extending concepts from other domains to family therapy. My interest in the theories of Maturana, Varela, and von Foerster did not arise from wanting to know whether a family could be considered to be an autopoietic system. I was simply struck by the elegance of the thought that had appeared in a field of inquiry close to ours and saw in it a source of inspiration for our own creativity.

If I had to list the main ideas that I have developed in the field of family therapy as a result of their work on self-reference, I would include the following:

1. *Structural coupling* is what occurs at the intersection of a system that is governed by its structure and the environment that surrounds it; this coupling is always circular. Extended to our field, this means that it is impossible to describe any therapeutic situation without including oneself, and what happens is always circular. I construct the family with its members and the family members construct each other and me.

2. *The therapist no longer has to use a preexisting conceptual map to explore the territory* constituted by the patient's or the family's pathology. The notion of territory is not meaningful in this situation. *We are concerned with the intersection of maps,* the therapist's and the patients', for it is here that the therapy unfolds. Perhaps I should no longer speak of maps and territories, because this implies that there is an objective reality, the territory, for which I can only create an inadequate map. It may be more relevant in this context to replace "map of the world" with "world view."

3. *In therapy, it is not truth or reality that is meaningful but the mutual construction of reality,* what Maturana and Varela call the multiverse. Different couplings cause different, but compatible, worlds to emerge. Solutions arising from these constructions are always pragmatic: the success of a therapy does not mean that the therapist was somehow "right," but simply that the construction that the therapist and the other members of the therapeutic system created "worked."

4. There is never in any situation only one possible solution. *There are many possible solutions,* depending on the interrelation between the members of the therapeutic system.

5. The elements described in chapter 2 as being capable of coming together, amplifying and changing the state of the family system, are always *self-referential.* These elements always belong both to the family system and to the therapeutic system.

6. *"Everything said is said by someone."* This statement of Maturana and Varela (1987, p. 26) reflects an ancient Talmudic tradition. In the Talmud even obvious statements are always attributed to someone. In the same way changes in the rules of a therapeutic system are always embodied in what individual members of the system say and do. What matters is what the members of the system experience in the therapeutic process.

7. *There is no such thing as the transfer of information.* Communication occurs in a process of coupling, in the intersection of constructions of the world.

8. *The problem of ethics is not eliminated* just because people are acting in a systemic context. Structural coupling preserves the importance of the individual; the environment does not take it away.

9. Varela's *emergence of the observer* is of fundamental importance. We will come back to it in chapter 6.

10. Finally, *paradox is central to life.* It is no longer something exotic, to be kept at a distance as if it were tainted by a whiff of the devil's sulfur.

At this point I can't resist the pleasure of recalling a wonderful commentary by Rashi, the famous scholar of the Bible and the Talmud, who lived in Troyes from 1050 to 1105. Exodus 20:19 (verse 22 in the King James version) says, "And the Lord said unto Moses, Thus thou shalt say unto the children of Israel, Ye have seen that from the Heaven I have talked with you." Rashi (1949) points out that there is another text, Exodus 19:20, which reads, "And the Lord came down upon Mount Sinai."

I do not know whether Rashi can be called a phenomenologist before the fact, but for him, as for a long tradition of scholars that includes in the present day my old professor Emmanuel Levinas, the relationship between transcendence and immanence was an important problem. It is not a trivial question whether the Law was revealed as a manifestation of transcendence—beyond the grasp of human experience and thought—or whether it can be seen as immanent, that is, within human experience.

Rashi offers two solutions to this contradiction in Exodus. He writes (1949, p. 221), "A third passage comes and harmonizes them: 'Out of heaven He made thee to hear His voice, that He might instruct thee: and upon the earth he made thee to see His great fire' (Deuteronomy 4:36)." Thus "His glory was in heaven and His fire and His might upon the earth." This first solution reminds us in many ways of Bateson's application of Russell's Theory of logical types (Bateson, 1970/1972): we can escape a double bind by separating its two terms and treating one as hierarchically superior to the other. But Rashi does not limit himself to this solution. He advances an alternative explanation: "He lowered the heavens and the heavens' heavens and spread them over the mount; and thus it states (Psalms 18:9), 'He bowed the heavens also, and came down.'" So we have a kind of Moebius strip or Klein bottle. Rashi offers us a solution in the form of a topological paradox.* God did not descend to earth and Moses did not mount into heaven, but God ordered the heavens in such a way that he could be on earth without being there!

For Rashi, paradox is not some kind of toy to entertain people with, it is the very center of the event that marked the beginning of the Jewish tradition, the very heart of the human condition.

---

*Topology is a branch of mathematics that deals with shapes. Two shapes are topologically the same if one can be distorted into the other. Thus a doughnut and a teacup, but not a doughnut and a saucer, have the same topological shape: if you make a clay model of a doughnut you can mold it into a teacup, but not into a saucer because of the hole. The Moebius strip is a peculiar form that has only one side. The Klein bottle has no separate inside and outside.

4
Therapists and Couples: Two Supervision Sessions

THE two supervision sessions transcribed here took place during a conference on couple therapy in Rome. The first was in French, with a therapist of Italian origin; the second was in English with a therapist who worked in the United States.

The first case will, I hope, let the reader see clearly how my model of couple therapy can be applied in a context that includes the different members of the therapeutic system. In the second case I partly abandon the model in order to work more directly with the therapist; the model does not help us understand how the system is stuck until the end of the supervision session.

This chapter and the next illustrate how psychotherapy can draw on the concepts presented in the first three chapters. Nevertheless, the second supervision session, called here "A Paradoxical Knot," shows how a supervision or therapy session goes beyond any model, however flexible.

From the Couple System to the Therapeutic System

MONY ELKAÏM: To start this morning, I'd like one of you to present for supervision a couple case you are working on. The supervision will allow me to present to you my couple therapy model.

Who wants to volunteer? [*A participant raises her hand.*] Good morning. What's your name?

PARTICIPANT: Bianca.

M.E.: I'm listening to you.

BIANCA: The couple is married and the husband is very oversexed.

M.E.: What's being very oversexed, Bianca?

BIANCA: I mean that he not only has sexual relations with his wife but also with other women.

M.E.: What's the problem?

BIANCA: His wife wants to leave him because of his infidelity.

M.E.: What infidelity?

BIANCA: The infidelity of the husband. His love affairs.

M.E.: Infidelity with respect to what?

BIANCA: With respect to the marriage, which should be monogamous. She says she has sworn before God to be faithful.

M.E.: This lady says, "My husband is unfaithful." Does she have other complaints about him?

BIANCA: Naturally there are also other complaints: her husband spends money on other women and he spends time with them.

M.E.: All I am going to tell you might not have anything to do with the truth and even perhaps with what is going on. The question is what I can construct as a model to try and understand a situation and to help people change. Therefore I am going to draw the following:

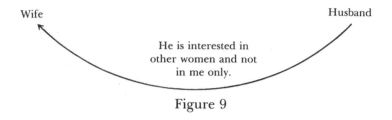

Figure 9

M.E.: Do you like that woman, Bianca?

BIANCA: Yes, I like her a lot.

M.E.: What do you like about her?

BIANCA: I like her because, unlike many women, she doesn't let herself get taken in.

M.E.: What you are going to listen to here is the story of the wife and the husband, and of Bianca and Mony. It is clear that everything that I am going to learn about this couple is what Bianca finds relevant to tell me. When Bianca says to me, "Unlike many women, that woman does not let herself get taken in," this in my opinion is extremely important. Why? Because both in couple and family therapy, what you see, what you describe, is what you construct in the process of seeing and describing. This means that what you say about people tells as much about yourself as about them.

In life every situation is self-referential, and this includes psychotherapy. It is impossible to imagine a psychotherapy which is not self-referential. Therefore what Bianca feels is what is going to create the unique link between her and this couple. It is what Bianca feels that will make this psychotherapy into one that bears her own signature. Bianca tells us, "Here is a woman who, unlike many women, does not let herself get taken in." Therefore something is being constructed here between Bianca's family of origin, the family of origin of that woman, between this couple and Mony Elkaïm, which we can already start to use and in fact are using.

What I am saying is, Rule Number One: when you see a couple or a family, listen to what arises inside you, lend your ear to that. Rule Number Two: don't use it as it is, because what you feel at that moment will very often lead you toward an even greater homeostasis of the therapeutic system. In general, the first thing that comes to your mind is very important because it shows you the unique bridge between the others and yourself; but at the same time you run the risk, if you follow it as you experience it, of allowing members of the therapeutic system not to question their deep-rooted beliefs. That is to say, to take up my model again, you run the risk of confirming both your world view and theirs, and creating a therapeutic system where each of you helps the other not to change.

Then what can we do? We can tell ourselves this: "What I am feeling is important, what I am feeling has a function and a meaning which is important in this context, both for them and for me, but I have to use it differently. How? We are going to see. Our task, beyond the supervision of the case, will be to consider the question, "How can the therapist work from the core of self-reference?"

Now let us go back to my couple therapy model. The woman says, if I understand correctly: "My husband doesn't pay attention to me."

BIANCA: Her husband claims that he loves her very much and that he does not do her any harm by going with other women.

M.E.: Therefore this woman says, "My husband is interested in other women and not in me only."

BIANCA: That's right.

M.E.:   Does she also say, "My husband is interested in other people—men and women—and not in me only" or does she only complain about his interest in other women?

BIANCA: Only about other women.

M.E.:   Perfect. We have here a cycle with a husband who spends time with other women and not with his wife only. Therefore my hypothesis is the following: if they have been living together for so long, it is because his behavior serves a useful purpose or she would have left him.

BIANCA: She left him several times but he would always go begging her on his knees to come back and live with him.

M.E.:   So why, when her husband gets on his knees before her, does she agree to come back? She could tell him, "I love you very much, my dear kneeling husband, but you go your way and I'll go mine." Why does she come back?

BIANCA: They have young children.

M.E.:   But in a similar situation other couples separate in spite of everything. Why don't they? My hypothesis is that if this woman keeps going back to this man, it is possible that already, in her personal history, in her childhood experience, she has lived similar situations where other women came before her and counted more than her. So I think her official program is, "I want to be the only woman who counts for my husband," while what I call her world view would be, "Other women come before me." Again my hypothesis would be that when her husband behaves the way he does, he has fashioned his behavior in a manner that confirms his wife's world view (*figure 10*).

But now we have to verify all of this and we can ask, "Would you tell me about a similar situation where you have had the impression that other women counted more than you did?"

BIANCA: I believe she has.

M.E.:   Tell us about it.

BIANCA: She was the second of three sisters. Her father was

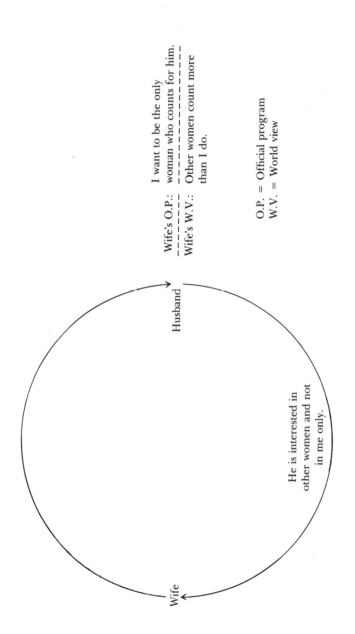

Wife's O.P.: I want to be the only woman who counts for him.

Wife's W.V.: Other women count more than I do.

O.P. = Official program
W.V. = World view

He is interested in other women and not in me only.

Husband

Wife

Figure 10 Wife's double bind.

often absent. The first and the last were the favorites of her mother and father, respectively.

M.E.: You are going to tell me, "Mony Elkaïm, in the systemic approach we have always challenged the idea of a direct causal link between past and present. And now you seem to be defending it. Aren't you going back to the old French saying, 'When the parents drink, the children have to put up with the consequences?' Even in the time of the prophets, Ezekiel (18:2) was challenging, 'The fathers have eaten sour grapes, and the children's teeth are set on edge.'

My answer is this. I do not believe that there is a direct causal link between the past and the present, but I do think that there is a complex cocktail of elements which are tied at one and the same time to the past and to the present, and that the historical elements cannot be underestimated. These historical elements do count, but they don't play a causal role.

My interest in the work of Ilya Prigogine and his team on open systems far from equilibrium was connected to the importance of chance and of what he calls amplifications and bifurcations, in these specific systems whose history does not have a linear evolution. History counts, but it is a noncausal history, a history where elements of the past are actively at work without necessarily being the cause of the present behavior. Is it clear?

PARTICIPANT: Can you spell out that point in more detail?

M.E.: For a long time in psychotherapy we have acted as if our present behavior were tied to the past in a causal way. In my opinion the choice does not lie between the assertion, "There is no link between past and present," and its opposite, "There is a cause and effect link between past and present." For me there is a third choice: "There is a link between the past and present, but this link is not one of cause and effect." It's like the relationship between the different ingredients in a cocktail. Each ingredient plays a role but none is the cause of the cocktail's flavor.

When I ask a question about the past based on the complaint that a person is making against his or her partner in the present, it is not because I think that there is a mechanical and automatic bond between the past and the present. In my opinion, the elements tied to our past are necessary but not sufficient. A particular context is also needed in order for those elements to be amplified to such an extent that they become dominant in a specific relationship. In one context, the elements can remain quiescent. In a different context, they can acquire such an important function within that system that they become amplified and then it can seem that they determine what happens. When a chord is touched within us it vibrates not only because it is our very own, but also because a specific context has been able to make the chord vibrate.

In the name of the principle of equifinality, which means that different initial conditions can lead to similar outcomes, the systemic approach has distrusted the logic of linear causality. This does not contradict the fact that the past can certainly count, but it does mean that the past is not the unique cause of what happens today. The elements of the past are among the factors actively at work, but they definitely are not the only cause. Can you see the difference? The cocktail's flavor can change if we change one of its ingredients; a therapeutic situation can be modified even when we don't walk the path of the past exclusively.

Let us come back to the case we are talking about. The lady says, "My husband prefers other women to me." I asked, "Is it possible that in her past she has experienced similar situations where other women were preferred over her?" And Bianca answered, "Yes, Mony, her parents favored her two sisters." If I use my model of a reciprocal double bind, it is possible that the wife is saying: "Love me and choose me as your wife. You swore before God that you were going to love me forever. Why do you now prefer other women?" But she is also telling herself, "Even if he behaved as if he loved me, in the end he would let me down, and I would feel again that deep pain I experienced with my mother and father with regard to my two sisters." Torn apart by this contradiction, she doesn't realize that she is saying, "Choose me," and at the very same time, "If you choose me, I will be frightened because I don't believe it's possible." This can explain why when "he comes back on his knees," she accepts him back.

PARTICIPANT: Are you saying that there is a deterministic relation between the woman's past and the man's behavior?

M.E.:   One could say that every time the husband chooses his wife, she dissuades him from doing so in an explicit or implicit way. Then gradually his behavior changes: he no longer shows her he prefers her. But again there isn't one single causal element. For the husband to go along with amplifying this kind of reaction, it has to fit both his own beliefs and the rules of the systems they each grew up in.

I would also like to give you another answer which would emphasize more the pragmatic aspect of my model. For that, I must tell you a story. One day when I was working as the director of a mental health center in the South Bronx, a very poor area of New York mainly inhabited at that time by Puerto Ricans and blacks, a Puerto Rican patient came to see me. I asked him what I could do for him and he answered, "What can you do for me?" I said, "If you tell me what I can do for you, I'll do my best." He was stunned. "Do you mean you don't know what's wrong with me?" he replied. "How would I know?" I asked. "You mean you want to help me and you don't know what is the matter with me?" "I am ready to do what I can for you," I said, "but I don't know what's wrong with you." He couldn't believe it and asked me, "Really, don't you know what's the matter with me?" I again answered that I had no idea whatsoever. Then he got up saying, "How can you help me then?" and with that he left. I actually thought that it was a joke that my colleagues at the mental health center were playing on me. I remembered a story that happened in Palo Alto: they had asked Don Jackson, who was a psychiatrist, to see a delusional psychotic who thought he was a psychiatrist. Do I need to say that the so-called psychotic was himself a psychiatrist and that he had been told the same thing about Jackson? And then I realized it was much simpler than that. I knew that in the South Bronx, certain Puerto Ricans who belong to the Pentecostal church often go to mediums when something is wrong. These mediums fall into a trance and describe to them the problem which is troubling them. It is only after this that the exorcizing begins. Therefore if I did not know what was his problem, how could I possibly be able to help him? The pastor of the Pentecostal church had to talk to the patient and tell him, "Elkaïm takes care of the material aspects of your problems and I take care of the spiritual side," before the patient would come to see me. He could accept at that point that I was incapable of guessing what his problem was.

What does this story have to do with your question? The connection is as follows. I know that the husband's behavior may not be directly tied to his wife's past. I do know that, but if I reframe his behavior as having a protective function in his wife's agonizing situation, I completely change the way they see their predicament. If she says to me, "I never had any experience as a child of being the favorite one, it's true; I never had any experience as a woman of being someone who counted or was preferred. I have counted, but only in second or third place, not as first"—if she says that to me, then I take that up again: "To what extent can we say that the husband has unwittingly found an original although painful way of showing his love, by behaving in an intolerable way that puts him in the wrong but may be protecting her?" When I make an intervention of this kind, the members of the couple are thunderstruck, but they cannot completely reject the connection I make. This allows them to live their drama differently. Do you see what I mean? My work is in a sense arbitrary, it doesn't lay a claim to the truth. What I am seeking to do is to create intersections of people's constructions of reality in order to help them change. In my opinion, it is possible that all psychotherapy works in this manner, regardless of its underlying theory.

Now, what are the husband's complaints about his wife?

BIANCA: The husband doesn't say very much against his wife. He complains that she torments him because of the situation between them and that she is not satisfied with the deep love he feels for her. He says to her, "I love you very much, but you must let me have my affairs because I can't make do without them." He is sincere. But I have to add something: he also says that he has taken her as mother.

M.E.:   This is interesting. I ask Bianca what the husband blames the wife for and she answers me that the husband blames his wife because she blames him.

BIANCA: The husband also has a history, a tragedy in his childhood. When he was five years old, his mother committed suicide by throwing herself out of the window.

M.E.:   Don't tell me too much, otherwise I'll lose the pleasure of finding things out for myself. It would be like a detective novel that gives the solution to the mystery on the very first page. Who would read such a detective novel? Leave me the pleasure of discovering what is going on starting from what they complain about in each other.

What else does the husband complain about in his wife?

BIANCA: The husband complains that his wife doesn't take good care of the house. He says, "You don't really take care of the house, you only take care of your boutique," and this is the only thing he can blame her for.

M.E.:   The observer cannot exist outside the observed system. He is present in the very system he observes. What I would like to do with you all and with Bianca, is to examine how Bianca emerges in the therapeutic system that she describes. For the moment, we are mainly taking into consideration the two members of the couple, but gradually we have to extend our work to include Bianca and myself, in order to better grasp the points of resonance that can help her work.

So the husband says, "My wife doesn't take care of the house but only of her boutique."

BIANCA: Because they have a maid who also takes care of the house. He also blames her for not taking enough care of the children.

M.E.:   And what else?

BIANCA: And that she is a little messy.

M.E.:   What else?

BIANCA: Sex is good enough.

M.E.:   Bianca never stops listing the complaints the husband makes about his wife and yet you can see that I keep on asking for more. This is because I need to feel something that moves me in order to construct our model. What I find will therefore be something appearing at the intersection of what seems important not only to Bianca and the members of the couple but to me as well. Having said this, it is possible that you might see a husband who answers, "I have nothing about which to reproach my wife, she is perfect." He might even persist in this way, "She is perfect and I am in the wrong." In that case you must look at what purpose it serves him to be in the wrong. What is the husband's world view that can only make him the bad one? And what is the function for this couple of the fact that she treats him as the bad one?

What else does the husband blame her for?

BIANCA: He blames her for wasting money and for spending a lot of money on her clothes. She replies that she spends a lot because he also wastes money, since his other women cost him a lot. He spends his money in nightclubs, restaurants, hotel rooms, whatever.

PARTICIPANT: Couldn't we say that she is not satisfied with his way of loving her, she is not happy with what he gives her or with the money she has at her disposal, as if that was one of the things the husband was complaining about? She is never satisified, she is never happy, she never gets enough of anything.

M.E.:   What you just picked up with such accuracy is that even if each of the things that the husband blames his wife for can seem minor, their common point is important. And the point is, "She is not happy." Can't we construct as a hypothesis the following double bind: "I want my wife to be contented with me," but "I have no experience of ever having contented those who were important to me?" We can draw this situation in the following way (*figure 11*).

What do you think, Bianca, of this hypothesis? That in his past he could never content those who were important to him?

BIANCA: Yes.

M.E.:   Tell me about it.

BIANCA: He had the terrifying impression that surely nobody was happy with him because when he was five years old his mother committed suicide by throwing herself out of the window. His father always pretended to him that she

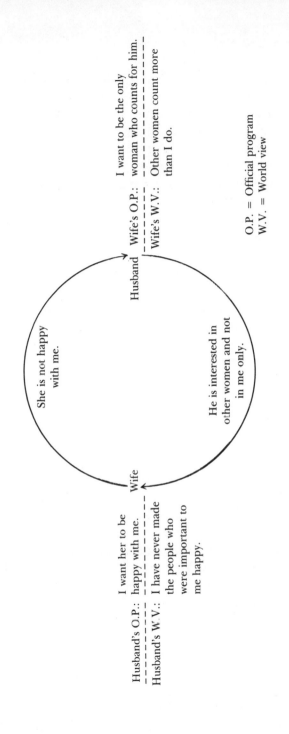

Figure 11 Couple's reciprocal double bind

had accidentally fallen, and all the other members of his family went along with that version.

M.E.:   Bianca, what makes you say that this man has lived this drama as if "his mother was not happy with him?"

BIANCA: He thinks that his mother was not happy with his father, who was also a ladies' man.

M.E.:   Bianca tells us, "Here we have a man who, at the age of five, heard that his mother had committed suicide." Did he ask himself, "Aren't I important enough to make her stay with me?"

BIANCA: Yes.

M.E.:   In addition, he can say, "My father made her life so miserable that she died." But he leads the same kind of life and his wife doesn't die, she leaves and she comes back.

BIANCA: She went into a depression and tried to commit suicide.

M.E.:   Now, thanks to what Bianca has been telling us, we can make the hypothesis that when the wife is not happy about the husband, she, without realizing it, confirms his world view, "Nobody can be happy with me."

Up until now all I have done has been very simple. The point has been simply to show you how I start from the complaints that one partner makes about the other in order to show the function of the behavior he or she wants to see changed, and how this behavior can neatly serve to "protect" the one who complains about it. I am showing you the functions of symptoms. The symptom as far as the husband is concerned is that his wife is not happy with him; the symptom as far as the wife is concerned is that her husband prefers other women to her. I see that a gentleman is raising his hand.

PARTICIPANT: Up to now all the interventions have been made by women. This must have a meaning with regard to the situation of this couple.

M.E.: What's your name?

PARTICIPANT: Fidel. [*"Fidel" means "faithful": laughter and a prolonged round of applause fill the hall.*]

M.E.: At the beginning of our work, we started from the complaints one person was making about the other in order to form hypotheses tied to the first person's world view. Later we saw how our hypotheses were confirmed. Now we must continue with the therapist and the supervisor to be able to understand how the themes that come up have resonances for them.

So tell me, Bianca, what do you think of that statement, "Other women come before me." Does that affect you?

BIANCA: Yes it does, it really does affect me.

M.E.: Don't say more than you want to say about it. If we were in a regular training group, we could go much deeper. Here we are at a seminar and we have a very different contract. Don't tell us anything more than you feel like.

BIANCA: I can still say that my father died when I was six years old. I had a sister and a mother who never remarried.

M.E.: What affects you about this theme of being preferred?

BIANCA: My father cared a lot for me because I resembled him a great deal. I was just like him and he loved me very much. I was the first. I was the one he preferred. But suddenly my father died when I was six and my sister five.

M.E.: What I hear Bianca say, correct me if I am wrong, is, "To have experienced being the favorite, the chosen one, can be dangerous." Is that what you're saying?

BIANCA: Yes.

M.E.: Then Bianca's world view may be, "It is very dangerous to be the preferred one." Something interesting can therefore happen between the wife and Bianca. The wife can be afraid for her husband to prefer her and wish for it at the same time. On the other hand, Bianca is afraid that if someone is the preferred one something very tragic can happen. We can see how Bianca's world view could mesh with the wife's world view in order to create a homeostasis in the therapeutic system and not just in the couple system. Is that clear to everyone? So then, now we are going to look at the other side. The husband says, "I am not able to bring happiness to those I'd like to make happy." Does this affect you?

BIANCA: It affects me because of his past. If he didn't have the past he has . . .

M.E.:   Are you saying, "This man lost a parent at the same age that I did and I feel very close to him? I am deeply affected by the thought that we both were unable to keep our parent alive?"

BIANCA: Yes, that's it.

M.E.:   Then at this point we can ask ourselves if what Bianca feels isn't resonating with the husband's world view to keep the therapeutic system in a homeostatic state. Our diagram then becomes the following (*figure 12*):

We have seen that Bianca has chosen with my help these specific themes only because they were equally touching for her. In supervision, my work would consist of making these points of resonance flexible enough for Bianca to use them as a gateway to a wide open range of possibilities for the members of the therapeutic system, that is, both for the couple and for her. You are going to say, "But Mony, couldn't we describe all that has arisen today with Bianca in terms of countertransference?" In my opinion, what we call transference and countertransference is only the tip of a much larger iceberg. What enters into play in supervision, for instance, is an intersection between elements tied to the therapist and to the couple, but also to the supervisor, to the rules of the institution where the therapy takes place, to the rules of the supervision group, etc. Here, by way of example, the term "chosen" can evoke many other references beside family elements.

The intersection between the therapist's construction of reality and those of the family members is certainly tied to their personal material, but it is in no way limited just to that [*see chapter 7*]. In certain situations, we need to stress the link with institutional rules, in others, the intersection with other contexts. Here, for instance, I found some points which commit Bianca to the couple and which naturally touch me as well, otherwise I couldn't have said anything about them. We can experience different things. What interests me is what is it that makes me experience these specific things, at this precise moment? What is the function, not only for myself, but also for the larger context to which I belong? And how can I use all of this? Time is rapidly running out and now we must say goodbye. Thank you very much to Bianca and to all of you.

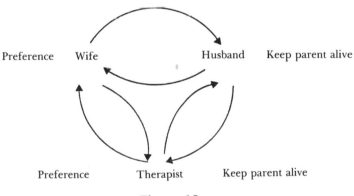

Figure 12

A Paradoxical Knot

M.E.: Who would be so kind as to come here with me to present a couple therapy case he or she is working on? [*A participant raises her hand.*]

M.E.: What's your name?

PARTICIPANT: Joan. . . . I am scared to do this.

M.E.: So don't do it. Why do you have to do it, Joan?

JOAN: Because it's good for me.

M.E.: Joan tells me, "I am scared to do this," and at the same time, "It's good for me." This is very important. We are already beginning to work. I have to keep in mind the possibility that what she is telling me can already be applied to a probable intersection between herself and the situation of the couple that she is going to talk about. I have no idea yet of the bond that might exist between a situation where what is good for her is just what she is scared of and the therapeutic system that she is going to talk about. But we shall see. Can you start presenting the situation of that couple?

JOAN: It's a cross-cultural couple. The husband is Burmese and he is forty-one years old. The wife is Thai. She came to the States when she was seven. They have four children. I had four sessions with them.

M.E.: When they first came to see you what did each have to complain of?

JOAN: The husband was depressed and angry at his wife. They were arguing with each other. They agreed on the fact that they were not getting along.

M.E.: Can you give me some more concrete examples of the reasons for their conflicts?

JOAN: He says that she does not listen to him.

M.E.: If I use my model, I would say that the husband's official program is: "I want her to listen to me . . ."

JOAN: ". . . and respect me."

M.E.: This could be part of a second cycle. But that's OK, let us work then with both "listen and respect." If I follow my model, I would ask this man a question to verify my hypothesis at the level of his world view. I would tell him: "Talk to me about the experience you have had in the past about being listened to. In your family of origin, who would listen to you?" Joan, do you know?

JOAN [*Thinking my question addresses her and not her patient*]: My mother primarily.

M.E.: Listen to me. Have you asked him this question?

JOAN: No, I haven't.

M.E.: Do you have any idea if in his past he would be listened to and respected?

JOAN: His sister and his mother . . .

M.E.: What would they do?

JOAN: They would listen to him.

M.E.: Did he say that to you?

JOAN: Yes.

M.E.: Therefore, he says that his sister and his mother would listen to him, but his wife doesn't.

JOAN: That's right.

M.E.: Do you listen to him?

JOAN: I do. And it really takes me a great deal of effort because he has difficulty expressing himself in English. When we talk, often we have to speak very slowly. I must speak very slowly and frequently ask him to repeat things he says on account of his very poor English pronunciation.

M.E.: So he says: "When I was young I was respected and I was listened to, but now my wife does not respect me or listen to me."

JOAN: Yes. In Burma he was respected also because he was a police officer.

M.E.: What I am doing here is trying to construct a model that allows me to help the members of the couple look upon their predicament with a different eye. Joan answers me what she thinks about what's happening to them without having been able to ask these precise questions to the members of the couple. For instance, you suppose that this man was respected because he was a police officer. But in my opinion, this is not obvious for the following reasons: Why has he become a policeman? Is it because that way he would be respected? What is this problem about respect all about? Since this couple is not here and I cannot send Joan back and verify this hypothesis, let us go on with another complaint.

JOAN: He says that his wife looks at other men and that makes him feel threatened.

M.E.:   Again, if I were to use my model, I would have to look, in order to have a better understanding of his complaint, at the experience of being threatened that he has had in his past. Have you explored that?

JOAN: No, I haven't.

M.E.:   Good, you went your own way with this couple and apparently my model cannot be of use for the moment. So, let's leave it aside. I am going to forget my model and just float with Joan and listen to how she has worked with this couple. Go on.

JOAN: This doesn't bother you?

M.E.:   My model is made to be forgotten. It is only a transitory tool. You do that [*blowing in the air*] and it goes with the wind. So I prefer to follow you. Tell me a story. Talk to me about this couple any way you want.

JOAN: I am not sure of how to present it.

M.E.:   As you feel like it, as you want.

JOAN: One of the concerns that I see and live with this couple is the cultural difference. The wife grew up in her Thai family and in that family system she had no independence whatsoever. Her family ran a restaurant business and she lived with them until she met her husband. They got married and her family had never spoken English before.

They only spoke Thai. And this man only speaks Burmese and very little English. When he married his wife, her family did not accept him. Her family expected him to work within the family business and not get paid for his services. And meanwhile he was working full time at another job. So she felt constantly torn between her family, which she had never really separated from, and this new alliance that she and her husband had formed.

M.E.: Why did they decide to come and see you?

JOAN: Because they were fighting all the time and they did not feel that was healthy to do in front of their children, but at the same time they did not know how to do otherwise. At the time they came to see me at the agency where I work, they were no longer living with her parents, they were living on their own.

M.E.: So they came to see you because they were arguing with each other and they felt it was not healthy to do this in front of the children.

JOAN: Yes.

M.E.: So why don't they fight when the children are not there?

JOAN: Because the children are always there.

M.E.: Then why don't they teach the children to accept that fights are part of life? Who needs to change a fighting couple?

JOAN: Often the children are present at the session and see what goes on between their parents.

M.E.: Why do you see children with the parents?

JOAN: One practical reason. . . . Well, I see families together and I don't always exclude the children. But to this must be added that there is no place for the children to be and nobody to look after them.

M.E.: Then you have a family with couple problems and with no space for a couple.

JOAN: Yes.

M.E.:   Why do you have to do couple or family therapy with them?

JOAN: Why do I have to?

M.E.:   Yes.

JOAN: I am not sure if I understand. They come and ask for help.

M.E.:   So just listen to them, but why do you want to help them? What's the use of helping people?

JOAN: What's the use of helping people?

M.E.:   Yes. They get better and they leave you. Who needs to help people learn how to leave you? I think it would be a good idea to keep people just happy enough so that they want to stay with us but not good enough to make them want to leave us. Who needs to have his children leave? It is this family's drama. The mother tries to leave her parents, but luckily their children will not leave them. They have been going to therapy with them. They haven't got a place to stay. They can't be left in the waiting room. They must stay with their parents in front of the therapist. So I think you should not help them, you should keep them with you. You should spend a lot of time with them, listen to them as much as you can, and give them no help whatsoever or try to make sense of their predicament. Because if this ever makes sense to you, perhaps one day it will make sense to them as well, and then they might get better and predictably they will leave you.

JOAN: Which does not bother me.

M.E.:   If people leave you it doesn't bother you at all?

JOAN: No.

M.E.:   How do you do that?

JOAN: Otherwise they'd stay forever and they'd never grow up.

M.E.:   Who needs to grow? Do you really want to grow?

JOAN: So you'd want them to be perpetual adolescents and never leave their parents?

M.E.: It's so much more pleasant when people don't leave you. Still . . . why are you in this business?

JOAN: I enjoy working with people.

M.E.: So then work with them, but do not cure them.

JOAN: I don't cure them, they cure themselves.

M.E.: Against you?

JOAN: Against me?

M.E.: Or with you?

JOAN: Some of each.

M.E.: Explain to me how you help them leave you.

JOAN: I don't know. That's a good question. I am not sure that one day they will grow up.

M.E.: If you don't think that one day they'll grow up, then there is no problem. Tell me, why do you want to speak about this case?

JOAN: They are not growing up fast enough.

M.E.: Why are they coming to see you?

JOAN: Because they want to stay together.

M.E.: Do you have something against fights?

JOAN: No, if they fight fair.

M.E.: Do you fight fair?

JOAN: Not always.

M.E.: What is fighting fair?

JOAN: I don't know. For instance, if I were to fight you, you shouldn't have your hands tied behind your back.

M.E.: If you were to fight me, would you hit me?

JOAN: Not physically. But I might with words.

M.E.: Where would your words hit me?

JOAN: Where you'd be vulnerable. Maybe in your heart.

M.E.: In my heart. And where else?

JOAN: In your eyes.

M.E.: Which eye, the right or the left?

JOAN: Both.

M.E.: Both eyes. And where else?

JOAN: Probably in your genitals.

M.E.:   My God! Luckily, I am not fighting with you. My heart, my eyes, my genitals, and where else? [*Laughter in the hall*]

JOAN: Isn't that enough?

M.E.:   So, then, fights can be incredibly dangerous. Yes. Maybe we should help people not to fight.

JOAN: We have to help people to fight.

M.E.:   Not to fight or to fight?

JOAN: Or not to fight?

M.E.:   I am asking you.

JOAN   [*After a silence*]: I think that in order to help them . . . when you ask me to define what fair fighting is, I feel really stuck.

M.E.:   Because is there no fair fighting?

JOAN: I think of how I fight with my significant other. This morning I have tried to have a fight on the phone ten thousand miles away and I am trying to think whether that was a fair fight or not.

M.E.:   Ten thousand miles away? I think he's lucky. [*Laughter in the hall*]

JOAN: I think he would agree with you.

M.E.:   I am glad to hear it, that at least makes two of us.

JOAN: But he didn't hang up on me.

M.E.:   And did you?

JOAN: No, neither of us did.

M.E.:   Do you mean then that fights can be good?

JOAN: I guess when I think about fair fighting, what goes on for me, Mony, is that no matter how angry you are, it is important for the other person to hear your anger. They may not accept it or understand it, but your anger should be heard. And this doesn't happen with this couple.

M.E.:   If you hit my eyes, my heart, and my genitals, what do I have left to hear with? My ears floating in the air?

[*To the audience*]: Now what am I doing here? Some very simple things. In a supervision, you never speak about a couple or a family, you are talking of an intersection between at least three systems: that of the couple, of the therapist, and of the supervisor. Therefore we are always looking for these intersection points, for these resonance points. Joan tells me: "These people come to see me and they complain of their fights." On the other hand, she does not tell me: "I see them as a family because I choose to do so," but instead "I see them as a family because that's what I usually do and moreover there's nobody to take care of the children." Therefore I am trying to work with her by amplifying certain aspects and by provoking her a little on the themes of conflict and separation. We shall see later how we can use that.

[*To Joan*]: Let's come back to our discussion on these fights. You have had one this morning and he survived.

JOAN: Yes, he did.

M.E.:   Have you survived as well?

JOAN: Yes.

M.E.:   So, then, that was a nice fair fight. Do you think that if he had been in front of you it would still have been a fair fight?

JOAN   [*After a silence*]: I don't think we would have fought.

M.E.:   I see. Therefore distance creates fights.

JOAN: It did in this case.

M.E.:   But in some situations, not to be separated can avoid fights?

JOAN: Yes.

M.E.:   And you want to help them learn how to separate without fighting.

JOAN: To separate from me . . .

M.E.:   I don't know.

JOAN: . . . and still be able to fight.

M.E.:   You want them to both be able to separate from you and to fight.

JOAN: I wouldn't expect that they are never going to fight again.

M.E.:   What if they fight and they hurt each other badly?

JOAN: But not to have fights in this family, Mony, means that one has to give in.

M.E.:   Can you give in?

JOAN: Can I give in?

M.E.:   Yes.

JOAN   [*After a silence*]: Not real easily. I used to give in all the time, but now I don't any more.

M.E.:   Have you found out how painful giving in is?

JOAN: Yes.

M.E.:   So, you should not give in?

JOAN: That's what happened in my family of origin.

M.E.:   What happened?

JOAN: That women always had to give in and let men win.

M.E.:   And don't you believe in that?

JOAN: No, because I have seen my mother give in all the time.

M.E.:   And?

JOAN: And what she didn't say made her very passive aggressive and she would get sick all the time.

M.E.:   So thanks to that, your husb— your father could say, "I have an aggressive wife," and feel at ease and be protected from being dethroned.

JOAN: Dethroned?

M.E.:   If I understand you well, your mother was giving in all the time, which would allow your father to win. On the other hand, she was passive aggressive, meaning that she would make his life miserable. This way he could be unhappy because she'd make his life miserable without realizing to what extent she was taking care of him by letting him win. This way he could have his cake and eat it too. Therefore your mother was suffering in order to protect him. This is one beautiful woman! Don't you think they should teach little girls in school to protect little boys?

JOAN: Moreover, that's where my father's expectations of me lay.

M.E.: Where?

JOAN: In that I should be subservient to my husband and be content to do anything that would allow him to succeed in his career.

M.E.: And is he very successful in his career?

JOAN: Yes.

M.E.: Not thanks to you?

JOAN: Pardon me?

M.E.: Not thanks to you?

JOAN: No, I think he is successful in his own right. He is in a totally different field than I am.

M.E.: If women must not give in, what are they supposed to do then?

JOAN [*After a silence*]: I think that they should stand up for themselves and get heard, understood, and respected.

M.E.: So women have to fight to be heard and respected. You are using the same words as the husband of that couple who asks to be heard and respected and who has the impression that his wife is neither listening to him nor respects him.

JOAN: Because in order to satisfy him she has to give up who she is.

M.E.: One moment. Do you think it is really possible to be heard and respected?

JOAN: Yes.

M.E.: Without giving in?

JOAN [*After a silence*]: I am not sure what "giving in" means to me. Giving in on what women are and giving up their own sense of self.

M.E.:   In your family, could you be heard and respected without giving in?

JOAN: Not in the family I grew up in.

M.E.:   The husband says: "She does not listen to me, she does not respect me. I want to be listened to and respected by her." The therapist tells us: "In my world view shaped by my family of origin, women can neither exist nor be heard or respected unless they give in." On the other hand, she says: "According to my official program, we should be able to be heard and respected without having to give in." Therefore the therapist cannot accept that this man has to give in in order to be heard and respected. Moreover, she cannot accept either that the wife has to give in to her husband's request, because then it's the woman who has to give in to be listened to and respected. Insofar as there's apparently no space between fighting and giving in, this couple seems destined to perpetual arguing if its members refuse to give in.

This shows us that we cannot speak of a couple and its world views without speaking at the same time of the world views of the therapist and of the supervisor. Everything that the therapist is telling us is the result of a structural coupling—to take up Humberto Maturana's term—a structural coupling which is formed between her, the couple she thinks she is describing, ourselves, etc. . . .

You surely have realized the futility of my research when I tried to go through a situation starting from the material that the therapist was providing me with about this couple. When I chose another path, through the relationship between the therapist and myself, and when, by provoking her tongue-in-cheek, I amplified certain situations that might have seemed absurd, something appeared. What appeared is the following: "We have the right to be heard and respected, but in my experience as a little girl, as an adolescent, and as a young woman, it seems to me that we have to pay a very high price for that, which is the same as saying that we are never either heard or respected. If I have to give in to be respected, it stands on evidence that I am not respected. What kind of respect is the one that is not offered spontaneously, but that we have to buy? On the other hand, if I pay to be respected, how can I be respected by someone whose respect I have to buy?" The elements making up the structure of the double bind are obvious: (1) I want to be listened to and respected, but in order to achieve that, I must give in. (2) To give in means that I am no longer listened to and respected.

At this point the double bind appears fully in all its unavoidable logic: I want to be listened to and respected, but it is not possible to be listened to and respected. The official program is: "I want to be listened to and respected." As far as the world view is concerned, it goes like this: "It is not possible to be listened to and respected." It is sufficient for the therapist's world view to tie up to that of the members of the couple to get as a result a homeostatic therapeutic system.

Thus we can better grasp the difficulty that has to be faced by the three members of the therapeutic system and how within this paradoxical knot there's no apparent way out of the dilemma that was put forward.

It is clear that the themes that I made appear, beyond the couple members and the therapist, are touching me as well, otherwise I could not have made sense of them. It is not a question of just recognizing something which is already known, but also of constructing a structural coupling between my experience and the environment that surrounds me. We constantly live in a self-referential and paradoxical world, it is the only one we have.

All I can do in this context with Joan is to show her that it is not by chance that she came out with the elements she presented me with and to make her see their role for both her and the members of the couple in avoiding change.

[*To Joan*]: So, then, you can float and maybe with a little bit of luck you will give in and you will not be either heard or respected, but it is perhaps the price that we have to pay for the life we live. Besides, is someone ever listening to us? When we call out to God, can He hear our voice? We are bound to get old and die; do you think that God respects us? Do you want to die one day?

JOAN: Yes.

M.E.:   It is not all that easy for me to have to give in.

JOAN: But you must give in.

M.E.:   But I must give in. . . . So then what seems interesting is what we can say about the human condition, which is not all that different from what we can say about couples. On the one hand, there is a kind of fairytale: we form a couple to be happy. A couple should be happy and not unhappy. And then the struggle starts: "It is up to you to make me happy, why do you refuse to do it?" If I live alone I am both prisoner and jailer and I can only blame myself for that. But if we are together, you are my jailer and I am your prisoner. And the more I suffer, the more I am angry at you. "Then just leave and let me finally be happy!" But as soon as you are gone, my God, I am in agony, I am so lonely, I come back to you and I ask you: "Forgive me and come back to me." And all the while I am telling myself: "I am completely out of my mind, why am I asking her to come back?" And you come back and we will start tearing each other apart again. . . .

Maybe couples have been created to better help us bear the human condition, to enable us to have someone to blame, someone who is responsible for our suffering. If we were alone, all we could do would be to yell at God. But God is a particularly difficult partner to drag into a quarrel. It's so much easier to do that with a wife or a husband! So, who knows, perhaps couples have been created to better help us go through the difficulties of existing.

Joan, Do you want to add something?

JOAN: Thank you very much, Mony.

M.E.: Thank you very much, Joan. Thanks very much to all of you.

5
Simulation of a First Session: Intrinsic Rules and Singularities

ONE of my favorite ways of training family therapists is the exercise called simulation. One student acts as a family therapist, others as members of a family. The therapist generally has no idea about the situation the simulated family is going to present. The student who plays the therapist and the ones playing family members experience a broad range of situations that can have a crucial influence on their personal and professional development.

One of the important aspects of simulations is the message they convey. We act as if it were not a question of pyschotherapy, and yet the purpose of the exercise is to train psychotherapists. And what if all psychotherapy were only simulation? Couldn't we consider every meeting between a client and a psychotherapist to involve an implicit agreement to participate in a rule-governed game called psychotherapy—a game in which calling the game itself into question is one of the rules? If so, simulation, above and beyond its underlying rationale, becomes the perfect metaphor for psychotherapy: a rule-governed framework in which what is important takes place not in reality but in the intersection of the constructions of reality of the various participants.

In the pages that follow, I would like to present a simulation that I led in France at a workshop I was co-leading with Carl Whitaker. There was an interpreter for simultaneous translation. As the simulation proceeds, you will be able to observe me as I apply many of the concepts presented in earlier chapters and will see how I engage in the two mutually influencing systems that I am a part of, the system of the simulated family therapy session and the broader system of the workshop participants.

It will soon be clear how the mutual construction of reality is fundamental to the process of therapy. Unique couplings between the family members and the therapist (especially the effect on the therapist of the gold streaks in the identified patient's sweater) appear. These intersections are enriched by the couplings between the rules of therapy and family rules such as the importance of "not believing in it." And we see these self-referential assemblages—composed both of seemingly trivial elements and of rules that will seem obvious to experienced family therapists—progressively enlarging. Finally, I stop the session when it seems that the process we have started will be able to continue without the therapist.

MONY ELKAÏM [*To the participants who are acting as family members*]: Good morning. Sit wherever you'd like. [*They arrange themselves as follows (diagram A)*]:

Family member 3	Family member 4
Family member 2	Family member 5
Family member 1	Family member 6
Mony Elkaïm	Interpreter

Diagram A

M.E.: What can I do for you?
FAMILY MEMBER 3: Well, you know, Joelle hasn't been eating. . . .
M.E. [*To the audience*]: I am going to ask you to tell me what you see. You have watched the beginning of something;

you have seen people come in; you have seen them sit down. What do you think about what has happened?

PARTICIPANT: A kind of group was formed. People came in and arranged themselves in a circle.

M.E.:   And then what did you see?

PARTICIPANT: You asked, "What can I do for you?" You didn't let the interpreter translate. The man began to reply and then you interrupted him. . . .

M.E.:   You're making me notice something very important. One of the systems here is the one made up of the therapist, the translator, and the family. The most comfortable place for me is here [*pointing to his place in diagram A*]. But if I put myself there with Judith [*the interpreter*] beside me, I am between you and the family members and you can no longer see them. If I sit here so you can see them [*pointing to a place that extends the semicircle*], I am no longer comfortable. I need to be an equal distance from all the family members. At the same time, I realize that there is only one microphone and I can't see moving back and forth so we can share it. I'm stuck. As far as I'm concerned, the most important person in psychotherapy is you, the therapist. If you're not comfortable, don't begin. And I'm not comfortable.

Now I hope you can help me find a solution so I can work with them. If I sit facing them, I make a barrier between them and you. I am going to look for a place where I can feel comfortable. Bear with me. . . . [*Puts his chair in different places.*] No . . . no . . . no. . . . So what am I going to do? I'm in a real bind. This is the only place I'm comfortable. And when I'm here I'm between you and them. What am I going to do? Help me a little, please.

PARTICIPANT: Lie down! [*Laughter in the audience*]

M.E.:   I'll try that [*lies down*]. No, I'm not comfortable that way. What am I going to do?

PARTICIPANT: Talk about it.

M.E.: I've *been* talking about it. I've been doing nothing but talk about it.

ANOTHER PARTICIPANT: Tell them that you're not comfortable the way things are set up now and see if you can work out with them a way to arrange things differently.

M.E. [*To the family members*]: What do you think? Let's work something out together. How can we arrange ourselves? [*The family members and M.E. move their chairs around until they come up with the following arrangement (diagram B)*]:

Family member 6

Family member 5

Family member 4

Family member 3   Interpreter

Family member 2   Mony Elkaïm

Family member 1

Diagram B

M.E.: That's better. [*To the participant who has just spoken*]: Thank you very much.

This lady said something very important to me. She said, "Why do you act as if the family didn't exist? Why did you act as if there were only us in the audience and you? The system isn't just us and you; it's us, you and them." And thanks to you, my dear, I'm beginning to breathe more freely now.

Well, I'd like to get back to the gentleman who was talking about how people arranged themselves . . . Who was saying that? Could you say a little more about it?

PARTICIPANT: Even when they changed places, the person on the left tried to recreate a circle.

M.E.: If this gentleman were in training with me, I would explore how the rule which he is bringing up is intrinsic to the whole therapeutic system and not just to the family system. I am not going to say to him, a priori, "Be careful, this could be a problem for you. You are running the risk of projecting your own issues onto the family." Instead I will exclaim, "What good luck! Here is something unique being constructed between you and the family around the subject of seating arrangements." But in order to do this I first have to establish what is involved in this unique bridge, this special connection, between you and them. My work as supervisor will then be to help you be able to use this specific gate. [*Returns to the simulation.*]

M.E. [*To the family*]: What can I do for you?

FAMILY MEMBER 3: I believe we've already told you we're here because our daughter has stopped eating.

M.E.: Yes?

FAMILY MEMBER 4: I'm really worried about it. Can't you help us?

M.E. [*To the audience*]: What have you seen?

PARTICIPANT: You're doing with them what you did with us.

M.E.: What I did with you?

ANOTHER PARTICIPANT: You made us do all the work.

M.E.: How am I trying to get them to do the work?

PARTICIPANT: By not saying much.

M.E.: As if I were talking just to you and not to them. I talk to them through my back.

ANOTHER PARTICIPANT: You let them think you can do something for them, because you say, "What can I do for you?"

M.E.: What I hear you saying is, "Dear Elkaïm, you open the session by saying, 'I am here for you.' So you define the context and you ask, 'Tell me what I can do.'" The way we start a session is very different from one therapist to another. If I say, "What can I do for you?" I am not necessarily talking of sickness or health. I am talking of me, Mony Elkaïm, and the fact that I'm going to try to use myself, to involve myself, for them. What else have you seen happening here?

PARTICIPANT: The father and the mother have put themselves in the middle, with the rest of the family on either side. It's interesting, the almost symmetrical arrangement.

ANOTHER PARTICIPANT: The father describes the problem, he speaks first. Then, when you leave some space, the mother begins to speak in a much more emotional way.

M.E.: You see already that if you follow that line of reasoning there is almost a distribution of roles between the father and the mother. If you start with the idea that the mother is emotional, you may create a system where she is in fact emotional. It is difficult not to participate in creating the thing we think we see. What else have you seen?

PARTICIPANT: What makes you think that the person who spoke was the mother?

M.E.: He's absolutely right. Just because a woman talks about a girl after a man has said something, it doesn't mean that she's talking about her daughter. We are always constructing. What else have you seen happening here?

PARTICIPANT: You're starting too fast. Before we even have time to hear these people begin to speak, you're already asking us to spell out hypotheses. I'd like for us to wait till things are clearer.

M.E.: When I am supervising a student's videotape, I always find in the first few minutes of the first session an enormous number of interactions between the family and the therapist. These seemingly trivial elements often determine the entire course of the session. You have mainly been paying attention to what has been happening verbally. Don't ignore the many nonverbal dances that have been going on up to now; they frequently determine and foretell what is going to take place later. As for the problem of clarity, the clearer things are the less space you have. Therefore I will express myself with greater and greater clarity, and the effect will be to plunge you into greater and greater confusion. [*Returns to the simulation.*]

FAMILY MEMBER 4: Joelle hasn't been eating and I am worried. We don't know what's happening, so my husband decided we should come and see you.

M.E.: Madame, can you introduce me to the people who are here?

FAMILY MEMBER 4 [*The mother*]: Freda, who is twenty; she works. Joelle, who is seventeen; she's the one who's not doing very well. Monique: she is nineteen and still lives at home. And so does Paula, who is sixteen. [*Participants are labeled in diagram C.*]

Paula

Monique

Mother

Father   Interpreter

Joelle   Mony Elkaïm

Freda

Diagram C

M.E. [*To the audience*]: What are your thoughts?

PARTICIPANT: The mother didn't introduce the patient first.

M.E.: Yes, that does seem quite important to me. What else?

ANOTHER PARTICIPANT: She only introduced her daughters.

M.E.: That is not uninteresting. It's as if the husband had to introduce himself. On the other hand, the husband had already spoken. Perhaps the mother was just introducing the family members who still hadn't said anything.

PARTICIPANT: Already that makes you think that the father is very alone.

M.E.: Again, you see how we each find our own way into the family. I personally didn't perceive the father as someone who is solitary or isolated. Already, different routes are opening up according to our own particular gates.

PARTICIPANT: What struck me from the very beginning was that the father seemed overwhelmed. It was as if he was turning the whole situation over to you.

M.E.: Again, here is a construction of what you see that corresponds to an intersection between you and the family. My intersections are slightly different.

PARTICIPANT: At the start the mother presented the idea of therapy as coming from the father. Also at the beginning of the session he was the one who spoke first.

ANOTHER PARTICIPANT: Within the family it seems there was a discussion between the wife and the husband, and then the husband presented the problem to the outside world. Another thing, the mother first introduces the two daughters who are both twenty-one. [*Cries of No! from the audience.*] I thought they were both twenty-one.

MOTHER: No—twenty-one, seventeen, nineteen, and sixteen.

PARTICIPANT: It seemed to me that the mother introduced her daughters in a way that was almost a caricature. She described them only by their ages and whether they worked or not.

PARTICIPANT: As they were talking, I noticed that they were all crossing their legs in the same way. And the father and Joelle had their arms in the same position. At that moment I thought that the father and Joelle were rather close to one another.

M.E.: What you are describing is in fact rather rare. Family members rarely all have their legs crosed in the same direction. Besides, you say, "There are two who cross their arms in the same way," and you infer that could mean that these two people are close. Again, you see how quickly we start the process of construction at the beginning of a session. [*Returns to the simulation.*]

M.E.   [*Addressing the identified patient*]: Your name, mademoiselle?

PATIENT: Joelle.

M.E.:   You have some pretty, glittering things on you [*referring to the gold streaks on her sweater*].

JOELLE: So what?

M.E.:   I don't know. It caught my attention. Perhaps it was because there is a part that glitters and a part that doesn't.

JOELLE: They didn't tell me I was going to be picked over from head to toe. Great, I didn't want to come anyway. It's a drag.

M.E.:   I don't know that I was picking you over from head to toe. It's more that I was wondering. I said to myself, "How funny, some of it glitters and some of it doesn't." And since I'm a dreamer . . .

JOELLE: The hidden face of the moon! Well, Dad, I'm willing to go through with this, but I think . . .

M.E.:   Just a moment, sir. Joelle, may I continue? Will you allow me to continue?

JOELLE: In any case, since I'm here, I don't have any choice. Even if I don't "allow" you, I have to listen to you.

M.E.:   That's not necessarily true, Joelle. If you want me to stop, I'll stop now, with pleasure. Do you want me to continue?

JOELLE: I don't know. I really don't know what we're doing here, sitting in a row like blackbirds on a telephone wire.

M.E.:   Well, what do you think we're doing here?

JOELLE: I'm not the only person here. You could talk to the others.

M.E.:   What's strange, you know, is that usually I do begin a session by talking to the others. But this time, it isn't my fault, or rather it is my fault—I plead guilty. It's true, the birds on your sweater and the way it glitters and doesn't glitter got my attention.

JOELLE: Now I'm beginning to laugh.

M.E.: And what's making you laugh?

JOELLE: They told me we're going to see a doctor. One more, 'cause we've already seen a lot of them. We're going to talk to him, and then . . . first, we have things to do . . .

FATHER: Mother, do you want to say something?

M.E.: Just a moment, sir. You're annoyed that I'm talking with your daughter?

FATHER: I'm annoyed because I can see you're upsetting her.

MOTHER: Maybe you could talk to her about something else besides her sweater? I don't know, I find that a little strange.

M.E.: How can I not think about the sweater when all I can do is think about it? [*Joelle whispers something to her parents.*] What is it, Joelle?

MOTHER: She's wondering if you're really a doctor. The way you are going about things is so strange. We've seen a lot of doctors, and you're the first to—I don't know, I don't want to offend you.

M.E.: Sometimes even I wonder if I'm really a doctor.

MOTHER: Don't ask me. You're the one who knows what you're doing.

M.E.: I'd love to know whether I'm doing the right thing. But I'm not convinced that I am.

MOTHER: She's starting to get a little upset. I don't know— maybe you could try telling us what we should do.

M.E.: Joelle, apparently your parents need to be reassured. Can you tell me what I should do to reassure them?

JOELLE: You always have to be told what to do.

M.E.: Yes . . .

JOELLE: Well, I don't know—anyhow, first of all I'm OK; and then, well, my parents are worried and then there are my sisters, and then we came here. And how long is this going to go on anyway? It's a real circus.

FATHER: Even so, don't be rude to the doctor.

M.E.: It's true that if you don't help me I'm a little lost, Joelle.

JOELLE: What am I supposed to help you do? Because maybe if I did start to help you out a little it would speed things up, because this is a drag. What am I supposed to help you do? You talk about my sweater, and then . . . I really don't think this is what my parents came here for . . . in my case I guess it's OK. I just don't know, anyway. . . . And you're bugging me. . . . You're making me feel aggressive and then. . . . Attack you, I could attack you and I could keep on doing it, but what are we supposed to be doing here? It's not that, anyway, we didn't come here to talk about that.

M.E.   [*To the parents*]: My problem is that I know you're here to discuss the fact that your daughter has an eating disorder. But all I can see is a sweater with some parts that glitter and others that don't, and a design of birds on it. And when you reproach me and say, "Work seriously," all I can see [*turning to Joelle*] is that pretty white ribbon in your hair. So I'm really bothered.

FATHER: Can't you see that she's five foot five and weighs eighty-eight pounds?

M.E.:   Joelle, what do you think of that?

JOELLE: I . . . [*starts to laugh*].

M.E.   [*To the audience*]: And what do you think of it?

PARTICIPANT: In the beginning the patient didn't look happy to be there. She sighed, she waved her foot about, she looked up and down. She sighed, and then you were able to get her to laugh.

PARTICIPANT: A couple of very commonplace things. You showed what was paradoxical between the way the family presented itself and the seriousness of why they were there.

PARTICIPANT: By speaking of the sweater you allowed the family to redefine the setting. It wasn't you defining the setting of the session, it was the family redefining it. . . .

PARTICIPANT: What I found interesting was that by not speaking of the symptom you kind of force Joelle to—you try to make her say what the problem is and you succeed in understanding a little bit, I think, what the function of the symptom is.

PARTICIPANT: I am really astonished at the way you, Mony Elkaïm, bring yourself in. You speak of your impressions, of your feelings, of what you experience when you see the sweater.

PARTICIPANT: You question Joelle, who tells you to talk to the sisters, to the others, and you continue to question her.

PARTICIPANT: Instead of saying she looks skinny and pale, you tell her she glitters and you make her blush.

PARTICIPANT: It seemed to me that when you were talking about the sweater she began to relax. She said, "We're starting to have fun," she lost her impatience. At that moment the mom told you, "We're not here for you to talk about her sweater." Then Joelle began to get aggressive again. And the mother pointed out to you that she was aggressive, that you were making her aggressive.

PARTICIPANT: I noticed that as Joelle began to relax, the father and mother got more and more agitated, as if they were the ones who really had the problem.

M.E.: I'd like to make a little remark. To begin with, I very rarely work this way with a family where there is an anorexic member. As a general rule, I'll explore the history of the problem. When did the symptoms begin? Then I'll study the context in which the problem arose and test hypotheses about its possible function on the level of the family system. I then paradoxically reframe the symptom as having a protective role for the family. Here, I was drawn in by the sweater. When I think of my own history, it reminds me of the first short story I ever wrote. It involved a student who was daydreaming while gazing at some bright flecks on the back of another student sitting in front of him in a lecture hall. At a certain moment he found himself drawn into the weave of the other student's sweater. It was a slightly crazy story, in the manner of Cortazar. And an intersection arose (I only realized this afterwards) between the story I had written and Joelle's sweater. At first Joelle seemed to be saying to herself, "What is he trying to show about me?" It was as if a fortune teller was going to try to say things about you based on the way you move your hands or your legs. As I begin to look like the one who has something wrong with him, I am the patient, I am the one who is saying, "I'm sorry, I can't manage to pull myself away from that sweater." At once the family joins against me, because I'm the patient and because freeing Joelle from her role as I.P. [identified patient] makes the parents uncomfortable. If I don't play the role of the crazy one at this moment, I run the risk of running counter to the system that they are proposing. Because if I don't ally myself with their way of describing the symptom, it means I'm not hearing what they're saying and I'm disregarding the function of the symptom. It's for this reason that I offer myself as patient. If there must be a patient, it can be me, it doesn't have to be the anorexic daughter. I'm enough of a heavyweight to take the role! Are there any more comments or questions before we continue?

PARTICIPANT: At the beginning, when the father presents you with the symptom, he more or less asks you to take his place to help his daughter. Your intervention seemed to irritate him and he made that clear to the mother.

PARTICIPANT: The sisters haven't said anything yet. [*Returns to the simulation.*]

M.E.   [*To the father*]: How are you putting up with me?

FATHER: Pretty well, I think. [*To his wife*]: And you?

MOTHER: I don't see what he's trying to get at. I don't think he understands very well.

M.E. [*To the mother*]:   When you lean forward like that, you seem so concerned, so open and eager to help. . . . I don't feel very good about the fact that clearly I'm not helping you, I have the impression that I'm not able to help you.

MOTHER: I have the same impression. I think we've gotten off on the wrong track.

FATHER: Maybe.

M.E. [*To a daughter*]:   You're very restless. What's your name again?

DAUGHTER: Freda.

M.E.:   Freda, can you help me a little? I'm totally lost.

FREDA: I think it would help if you would explain a little how you work.

M.E.:   To tell the truth, I don't really know how I work.

FREDA: But I think we came here with a request. Now I think it's up to you to tell us what you can do for us.

M.E.:   Can you help me understand the request that brings you here and what you expect of me?

JOELLE [*To Freda*]:   You want to tell him what we should do?

FREDA: I think—I can say what I think, can't I? It's my parents who are worried about Joelle. That's what's bothering us.

M.E. [*To the audience*]:   So, you see how Freda redefines the problem. For Freda, the problem isn't her sister's anorexia, the problem is her parents' worry. Freda speaks in a rather ambiguous way, so we can understand that it's the parents' worry that's the problem, as well as the fact that her sister doesn't eat. [*Returns to the simulation.*]

Can we keep on going around the room so I can get an idea of what you expect from me?

PAULA: I'm glad to talk, because I'm fed up . . . because when she doesn't eat any more, I just get hungry; and I wonder what the hell we're doing here.

JOELLE: If you don't like it, you can leave.

MONIQUE: I think this is going on a little too long, too. I think Joelle is being hassled too much. She's fine like that. I wish they'd leave her alone sometimes. They're on her case all the time: "Eat, eat, eat." But she's not doing so badly.

FATHER: The internist said if she lost four more pounds they'd have to hospitalize her on an emergency basis. We mustn't forget that. After all, we're talking mortal danger.

M.E. [*To a daughter*]:   What's your name?

DAUGHTER: Paula.

M.E. [*To the remaining daughter*]:   And you, what's your name?

DAUGHTER: Monique.

M.E. [*To the mother*]:   I'm really in a bind, because I understand that this is a truly serious problem. And apparently nobody before me has been able to help you. And why should I be able to help you? Why should I be any better than the others?

MOTHER: That's true.

FATHER: I have a question. Don't you care that our daughter could die?

M.E.:   Of course I care. . . . But you talk as if my caring about what happens to your daughter would mean that I can help you. First we have to see if I am sufficiently competent. Maybe I'm just not competent enough to help you.

FATHER [*To his wife*]:   Didn't the doctors say that it was only Dr. Elkaïm who could get us out of this?

M.E. [*To the audience*]:   See how fascinating this is. Here is a family which has seen numerous doctors without any results, as they told me in the beginning. And it was easy to see from the start they didn't think there was much reason why I should succeed. The more I made my incompetence explicit, the more they became competent themselves and the more they demanded that I be competent. It was as if they were saying, "We want to be helped, but we don't want a competent doctor." That made me think of the father's role. In spite of his privileged position, he doesn't succeed in helping his daughter. If I take the position the family members seem to be offering me, there is the risk that the father's position will be even further reduced. From the moment that I respond to both levels of their demand, when I offer myself as someone who wants to help but wonders if he can, I free up the family to be more flexible. The danger would arise if I became competent, because then I would only be responding to one level of their demand. I am going to see how, while remaining incompetent, I can still help them. [*Returns to the simulation.*]

M.E. [*To Joelle*]:   Hello, Joelle. Your father really affected me.

JOELLE: Like the sweater?

M.E.:   No, much, much more. He reminded me that beneath your smiles, beneath your niceness, some dramatic things are going on. Can you tell me about them?

JOELLE: I don't know. I don't see anything dramatic. You heard my sister: she said there was nothing special happening.

M.E. [*To the father*]:   I see you're shaking your head.

FATHER: Yes. I can't believe what I'm hearing!

M.E.:   You can't believe it? Go on please.

FATHER: What is there to say when Joelle claims there's no problem? Every meal is a battle!

M.E. [*To the mother*]:   Excuse me?

MOTHER: Yes, doctor.

M.E.:   You say, "Yes, doctor," as if you were saying, "What's the use of all this?" Right?

MOTHER: Yes, I've been wondering that. I'm a little disappointed at the way you're going about things. I thought you'd be more active.

M.E.:   How?

MOTHER: I don't know. To be perfectly honest, I came here because my husband thought it would help. Personally I never believed it.

M.E. [*To the audience*]:   Listen. What she's saying is very important. She says, "My daughter is in danger of dying," and also, "I don't believe that anyone can help her." This can be understood as, "My daughter may die and I don't dare hope that the situation can change," or even more simply as, "I don't believe this can change." If the therapist calls attention to what she is saying, it's probably not going to be very helpful, because she's likely to get angry at him. For me, the fact that the mother is unable to believe that the situation can change reminds us that the symptom has a function, that it is useful, that it is important. [*Returns to the simulation.*]

M.E. [*To the father*]:   I am very touched by what your wife has just said. What I heard was, "I want so badly for my child to get better, but I don't dare believe that it's possible because I'm so afraid that it won't work" [*the mother nods her agreement*] or again, "I'm so afraid of believing that she could get better and that she won't, that I no longer dare believe that things are going to work out." [*To the mother*]: You're nodding yes.

MOTHER: Yes, I can see that you're really with me.

FATHER: You've understood our feelings very well.

M.E. [*To the mother*]:   Are you the kind of person who would rather believe that something you want won't happen for fear of being disappointed if it doesn't?

MOTHER: Yes, all the time.

M.E.:   Give me an example.

MOTHER: I don't know. Well, when they go to school, I'm always afraid that they're going to fail. I'd rather think that they'll fail . . .

M.E.:   I see. Can you give me another example?

MOTHER: My husband was in line for a job. Well, he got it, but I was always afraid that he wouldn't. Up to the last minute I preferred to think that he wasn't going to get it.

M.E.: What do you think, sir, about what your wife is saying?

FATHER: That's exactly how she is. If we're having guests in, she keeps saying she's going to spoil the dinner and then it's delicious.

M.E.: Joelle, what do you think about what Dad and Mom are saying?

JOELLE: Oh, my mother cooks very well.

M.E.: I hear what you're saying. And what do you think when they talk about being afraid the things they want won't happen?

JOELLE: You were using the word *dramatic* a little while ago. That's what it is, all drama. Mom is always convinced that something catastrophic is going to happen. Always. I'm not causing the drama: it's always like that. She's just told you so.

M.E. [*To the audience*]: We are now at a point when they are offering me the following possibility: "Mony Elkaïm, are you ready to ally yourself with us in a context where you too fear the worst?" That means that I too should behave as if I weren't at all convinced that I was going to succeed. But how to make this joining into something which will be a source of flexibility for all of us? Help me. How am I going to get out of this?

PARTICIPANT: Could you suggest to them how hard it would be for you to eat at their house, with this lady who is afraid of ruining the meal and you who are also afraid that she'll fail, and how it would still work out, given all this?

M.E.: In the first place, I don't like to go eat at my patients' homes; and if I do go it will definitely be terrible. It will be so terrible that I'll get an upset stomach from it and become sick.

PARTICIPANT: Could you ask them to play act a meal?

M.E.: In our field there is a gentleman called Salvador Minuchin whose secretary asks the family members to give her orders for a meal. The sessions are usually held at noon. He works with what happens at the meal. But that's Sal Minuchin. That's not Mony Elkaïm.

PARTICIPANT: Could you work around what you both fear the worst, the family as well as you?

M.E.:   Each one of your suggestions is important and useful, but there are some which I feel I could carry out—like what you just said to me now—and there are others which I can't see myself trying. It's something that's equally important in training. If you're my student, it's not enough for me to say to you, "Here's what you can do." You also have to be able to find something that's close enough to your way of thinking so that you'll be drawn to it. So you said to me, "How can I utilize what I fear the most?"

PARTICIPANT: Yes, work with what you fear the most, together, you and the family.

M.E.:   Thank you. Who else?

PARTICIPANT: I would have liked to talk about my fears that the therapy couldn't succeed.

PARTICIPANT: Why not work with the mother, with the anxiety of the mother, who may be the real I.P.?

M.E.:   You could do that if you constructed the situation that way. When I see a family, I prefer to think in terms of what the whole family does rather than what any individual does by him or herself. Moreover, if there has to be a patient, I prefer it to be me.

PARTICIPANT: Why don't you take her place?

M.E.:   The problem, if I take her place, is that I will be acting as if I could be in her place, which is impossible, because we are never in anyone else's place. I'm going to create my own place in our system. I can be the patient in my own place. That will change the distribution of roles in our system, but it will be my own place, not hers. [*Returns to the simulation.*]

M.E.:   You see, father, mother, your daughter Joelle is saying to me, "I am very sensitive to what my parents are experiencing. My parents are so eager for the best for us that they don't believe it can happen and spend their time fearing the worst." As a therapist I hear very clearly that she is saying: "They don't have to fear the worst, the worst is here. I am the worst. And you don't have to be frightened. It's already here." But I'm frightened. I'm frightened because it's a very painful and very dangerous situation. It's as if Joelle were trying to say: "Stop being afraid. What could be worse than what's happening to me?" And I say to myself, "How can we let a girl of her age take the position that she is taking?" So for me it is perhaps her own individual way of showing how she cares for you when she says: "There is no longer any reason to be afraid. I am going to do such a job for you in that department that morning, noon, and night you'll have something to be afraid of." And if my slightly off-the-wall idea isn't entirely wrong, maybe what looks like her refusal to eat is really her own special way of loving the two of you. But what a strange way of loving! What do you think, Joelle?

JOELLE: I've already said everything I wanted to.

M.E.: I agree. What do you think, sir?

FATHER: So you're saying that deep down you can tear people up because you want to protect them?

M.E.: You see, what strikes me, sir, is that already you are saying, "I'd rather I was the guilty one, so that my daughter could breathe easy, so that it would be my fault that she isn't well." It's as if you were saying, "If someone has to be guilty, it will be me." [*To the mother*]: What do you think?

MOTHER: It's sort of what you're saying: it's our fault if Joelle has this problem.

M.E.: I can understand why you're saying that, and it shows how badly I've expressed myself. And that shows how I always have to think of the worst. Because what you just said never even crossed my mind. But I realize now that I put it so badly you could take it that way. And how can I be a therapist if I put things so badly? If I say things that are not just foolish, but really stupid, things which cause harm and hurt people . . .

JOELLE: He's worse than you, Mom.

MOTHER: Yes, he really seems . . .

FATHER: Well, I don't know, doctor, in the end I'm not sure that what you're saying is all that foolish.

[*M.E. Sighs.*]

JOELLE: Well, what are you afraid of, after all? We're used to it at our house. Mom is afraid of everything, of what happens, of what doesn't happen, of what could happen—morning, noon, and night, all the time. So what are you afraid of?

M.E.: First, I am afraid for you, and then I am afraid of not being able to help you. And it's so important to help you that I'm really scared of not being able to do it. And I would detest myself for raising the hopes of your parents, of your family, and then not being able to help. That's what I'm afraid of.

FATHER: I don't agree with what's being said about my wife. She is warmhearted; she has raised the kids in love, not in fear. Yes, you do have your own fears, but I think you've always been reassuring to others.

MOTHER: Are you playing some kind of game? Do you really believe it's as serious as that? I'm beginning to wonder.

M.E.: I think that your daughter is in a potentially dangerous physical condition, and I wonder how I will be able to help you. My fear is that I will not be able to help you.

MOTHER: Do you think you're taking this very seriously, knowing the situation we're in? You say you're not sure you can help us. . . . either the situation is grave or it's not.

M.E.: You're right. I take it so seriously that I can only work with you if I say: "I am not sure I can help at all. Perhaps you should keep asking yourselves whether you shouldn't change therapists."

JOELLE: No, it's fine the way it is.

FATHER: You're like us. You foresee the worst so it won't happen.

M.E.: I would certainly be very happy if it didn't happen. So, I have a proposal to make to you. As Joelle has seen so clearly, I am a person who is always asking for help. And I really do have the impression that without your help I won't be able to do anything. Without it, I don't dare begin. I don't know. I don't even know what I could say to you.

JOELLE: I'm beginning to be hungry now.

M.E.: Oh, excuse me. I forgot to say that I get equally afraid when things change too quickly. And when you say you are hungry, I am a little afraid. . . .Excuse me, sir?

FATHER: I was saying to my wife that you're a character.

M.E.: Well, if in spite of everything you want to see me again, I'm willing to meet you again without promising anything, and we'll see. Goodbye. [*Shakes hands with and says goodbye to each member of the simulated family.*]

I'm going to ask the members of the simulated family to share with us what they experienced before we have a more general discussion. [*To Paula*]: Would you begin?

PAULA: It's rather difficult to say, because at certain times I was following what you were saying, so I was playing the part, but other times I wasn't. I wanted to play the part of someone who wasn't that bothered by the problem of her sister's anorexia. In the beginning, I was perhaps pretending not to be really interested in what was going on. But even though I was pretending to have this attitude, I found myself caught up in it. So in spite of the role I had decided to assume, something happened. The longer the session went on, the more I began to believe that something would happen. And now that the session is over, as a member of the family I still have a request for you. I want the therapy to continue. That's all I have to say.

MONIQUE: In the beginning I thought I would get more involved, and then in the end I just let things happen. It seemed to me that most of what was going on was between the par-

ents and my sister. I withdrew a little. But to tell the truth, if
we were going to continue, I would come back for the next
session.

MOTHER: Speaking for myself, at the beginning I was very
uncomfortable because I told myself that I was going to have
to play a very important role. And then little by little, because
of the way the session unfolded, I felt less and less important.
As the session proceeded, I felt my load getting lighter, but
at the same time some part of me was troubled by that. I still
wanted the problem to continue a little bit. My importance in
the family came from Joelle's problem and that importance
was reduced to the extent that Joelle's problem was on the
road to resolution.

FATHER: I believe that for me there were two phases to the
session. At first, a phase when I was furious because Joelle
was not the identified patient; then a second phase when there
were things that made me angry and other things that pleased
me. I was angry at my daughters, who seemed to be saying
that the problem came from us. They were betraying us, in
no uncertain terms. I was angry because my wife was being
attacked: I could feel how unhappy she was beside me. And
on the other hand I was extremely relieved when Mony highlighted his own incompetence. In the beginning I was very,
very frightened of him, and then he didn't threaten me any
more, and finally he opened up some perspectives that I
hadn't thought of, and I wanted to continue.

JOELLE: I'd like to talk about how I experienced the session and
also about what I gained from it. In the beginning, in order
to play Joelle the anorexic, I tried to remember what I thought
I had been able to see in my anorexic patients. At that moment
the notion of the family system was a total fiction to me. And
then progressively I really found myself in the role that the
game had assigned me, and it was no longer a game. What I
mean is that at several points it seemed to me that my father,
my mother, and myself were trying to thwart what Mony was

doing, because of my practice, of my profession—I am a psychiatrist. And then after a certain time it wasn't possible any more. It was at that moment, without a doubt, that a new system involving both the therapist and the family came into being; that's how I understood it. That seemed very, very important for my practice. The new system, the therapeutic one, doesn't form immediately. But it has to come into existence sooner or later, even in a simulation.

FREDA: I was annoyed at first because they were talking about a sweater instead of about the problem. And also because the therapist was using big words about feelings, which I couldn't believe in. Later, I was a little bored, but at the same time a little relieved, because the therapist was concentrating on my parents. So at the end I was ready to come back for another session, yes; but without hope.

M.E.: OK. [*To the audience*]: Now I'd like to throw things open to general discussion. Who wants to say something? Who wants to make a comment?

PARTICIPANT: I'd like to know what Joelle experienced when Mony Elkaïm spoke to her about her sweater.

JOELLE: It's complicated. I was both annoyed as a patient and amused. I was still in the first phase of the session, when I wasn't yet involved. But the challenge was too strong for me to be able to remain myself looking in from the outside, and I quickly put myself in the place of the anorexic.

M.E.: With that sweater I understood that I was speaking, although not intentionally, of a metaphor: the parts which were shining and others which were not. I saw those birds that wanted to fly away, and I sensed that something else was being said without my having to be explicit about it.

PARTICIPANT: I was surprised that you took a one-down position with the parents. I would like to know if you usually do that, if you usually put them in a one-up position and ask them what solution they could find for what is going on in the family?

M.E.:   What's interesting is that I'm most likely to take a one-down position in simulations, in large groups. Why? Because you come here to hear people who apparently have quite a lot of experience and there's already the risk you will think they know more than you do about what you can do. For me, it is extremely important, when you come here, that you discover more about your own possibilities than about mine. What can I do to demonstrate your possibilities? By giving you the example of a therapist who wants to take a very minor role. So what do we find? The more unimportant I make myself, the more important I become. And so there is this incredible situation. They say to me, "Be important! Assume the leadership we expect of you, as therapist, as organizer of this workshop." And I reply: "You really want me to lead you? Since when can someone heal someone else? Since when can someone teach something new to someone else? I can only help you find in yourself what is already there. I can only help you see what is right in front of you." And this is how, often, with large groups, I become as important as I possibly could be by being as unimportant as I possibly can. Who wants to say something?

PARTICIPANT: I would like to go back to your remarks at the very beginning on the notion of constructing reality. I was saying to myself that this was a simulated family, that they came to us with a sort of framework, that they had planned a little bit who they were. And then as things happened I think they began constructing something different from what they brought to us in the beginning. I would like you to talk about families which are not simulated, and to this aspect of construction, perhaps even of creation, that can occur in the relationship with the family.

M.E.:   Simulated families are generally more resistant to change than real families. The members of a simulated family try to maintain the scenario they have constructed. But since the game is called psychotherapy, at a certain moment they find themselves changing. This means that for me there are certainly differences between a simulated family and a real one, but change occurs in both cases. And in both cases I'm wary of change. One doesn't speak of rope to the family of a hanged man. One doesn't speak of change to people who need things to stay the same. In addition, I am so much in love with the extraordinary beauty of the architecture families and couples construct that, sometimes, I don't dare alter this extraordinary edifice. At such times I say to myself, "But what if they simply lived with the situation?" or "Who am I to interfere?" When, as in this case, the symptom is painful and dangerous, I'm completely torn between this "Who am I to interfere?" and the risk that the symptom is imposing on the patient and the family. In the present situation, I tried to respect the existing balance by proposing myself as the symptom, which obviously changes the balance and so opens up new possibilities.

Many thanks to the members of the simulated family. Many thanks to all of you.

6
From the Therapeutic System to the Assemblage

In chapter 4 I emphasized the importance and usefulness of what the therapist experiences while interacting with the couple. Obviously I could have applied the same line of reasoning to the experience of each member of the therapeutic system.

What a husband or wife experiences in the session has a function not only in relation to the spouse, but also in relation to the therapist's world view. The feelings that arise in one or another of the members of the therapeutic system do not come uniquely from that person's own history. What is felt in itself is unique, but it is amplified and maintained by its context; what the protagonists in a therapeutic system experience is both linked to themselves and not reducible to them. It is far richer to think about the function and meaning of the feeling experienced in relation to the whole system than to limit one's hypotheses to purely internal dynamics.

Four Situations

The four situations I describe next will allow me to introduce a concept I call *resonance*. This concept helps me underline the importance of contexts that are linked to the members of the therapeutic system but not reducible to them.

Caught between Two Fires

In this supervision I began to develop the concept of resonance. The student I was supervising, who came from another country, was director of education in an institute for specialized professional training, a school where sixteen- to nineteen-year-old girls boarded during the week. The director of the school asked my student to take charge of a special situation, in collaboration with the school psychologist. He had just received a telephone call from the maternal grandmother of one of the boarders, asking him to get the girl to stop hitting her mother when she was home on weekends.

It appeared that the mother was extremely dependent on her own mother. The grandmother, for example, drove her to the school when she wanted to visit her daughter. According to my student's information, the mother's personal space was very limited. She was constantly being intruded on by her daughter and her own mother. She was caught between two fires.

My student described in detail how he in turn was stuck first between the director and the teachers and then between the teachers and the psychologist; he too felt as if he was caught between two fires. When I pointed out the parallel between this and the situation in the family, he told me that similar conditions used to exist in his family of origin.

His mother was his father's second wife; there had been three children by the first marriage. He was the one that his half-sisters and half-brother came to when they wanted to ask something from the parents, particularly the father. Besides, when a problem arose between the father and the three older children, the father always blamed him. He was also the child who had to intervene with his parents when they were fighting. So in the same way, he felt stuck between the siblings and the parents, between his mother and his father—caught between two fires.

I was at the time particularly sensitive to this intersection between three different systems. I realized that what had come up in the supervision was equally linked to the intersection of the student's world view and my own. Belonging like him to different cultures, having been like him caught between two fires at different moments of my existence, it was clear to me that I had to take into account the self-referential aspect of this construction.

Being There and Not Being There

The next supervision took place in one of my ongoing training groups. My student showed a videotape of a session with a father and his eighteen-year-old son, who was described as being psychotic since the death of his mother ten years earlier. The therapist lived in another country and had to travel in order to pursue her training.

At the beginning of the tape, the father never stopped complaining and expressing the bitterness he felt at the fruitless attempts of the doctors, who for ten years had been unable to help his son. He protested that he had always helped the other members of his family, but no one had ever helped him in return. Everyone had disappointed him. He didn't think he could expect anything from my student: he had the feeling of being there and not being there at the same time.

As I watched the tape, I noticed that the therapist seemed to be overcome by an increasing exasperation. The more she heard the father repeating how no one could do anything for his son and for him, and how alone they felt, the more annoyed she seemed. I asked her then if she remembered what she had experienced at that moment and she replied, "I was there and it was as if I wasn't there," although she stated that it was hard for her to associate this reaction with any experience that was important to her. I suggested that she think of a color and when she answered, "Amber," I suggested that she muse on that color and tell me what came up for her.

She described herself at the age of five, at the door of her father's office. He was asleep in his armchair, in front of his work table and surrounded by wooden cabinets full of books bound in yellow gilt leather, the color of amber. She would have liked to speak to him, but she didn't dare wake him up— she was there and it was as if she wasn't there.

Then she remembered another situation when she was about the same age. Looking for some cloth to dress her doll in, she opened a drawer in one of her mother's wardrobes. Inside she saw some prettily colored material: it was one of her mother's most beautiful dresses. She took it and cut it up. Shortly after, her mother found out what she had done and began to reprimand her severely. While the little girl was being scolded, there was a knock at the door. It was one of her friends and the friend's mother, who were coming to get her to go out and play. She was in tears, but her mother acted as if nothing had happened. Commenting on this episode, she declared: "For my mother, the image she gave to other people was more important than what I was feeling. She didn't see me. It was as if I wasn't there."

Up to this point, the situation is very similar to the ones I described in chapter 4. We see how a given theme can prove as important to the therapist as it is to the family members, and how their world views can interact to maintain the homeostasis of the therapeutic system.

But then I learned that the psychiatrist who was chief of the service where this family was being followed was planning to leave and that there would be no more family therapy consultations. The fact that my student was herself a psychiatrist and also saw families didn't change the decision in the least. Once again, she was there and it was as if she wasn't there.

Then we discussed her experience in the supervision group. Her professional obligations kept her in her own country at certain periods, and it happened that in the last months these periods corresponded to the times when she was supposed to participate in my training sessions. Now I had refused to change the dates of my workshops for her and again she had experienced my refusal as confirming that she didn't count, that she was there but everything happened as if she weren't there.

Thus I discovered that the same rule can apply at the one time to the patient's family, to the therapist's family of origin, to the institution where the patient is being seen, and to the supervision group. Here again I want to emphasize that this intersection between different systems doesn't exist in reality, but flows from a *mutual construction of reality* created by my student and myself in the supervision group.

Having a Place

The next supervision took place in a training group at the Institute for Family and Human Systems Studies in Brussels, of which I am the director. I am personally involved in the group only two days a year; the other sixteen meetings are led by colleagues.

The student who was asking to be supervised wore her hair in a peculiar way that didn't fail to get my attention—it hid half her face, which, as it happened, was very attractive. Here is the situation she was faced with.

A school director had asked the establishment where she

was working to take charge of a student who had problems, adding that the student was absolutely unwilling to meet with a psychologist. The members of the therapeutic team assigned to this establishment had no precise place. They functioned as if they were interchangeable. It was clear that they could not lay claim to a place of their own. It was also clear that the director's request left no room for maneuvering.

Contacted by my student, the mother replied that she didn't see any problem in the young woman's visiting her son at their home as long as she carefully hid the fact that she was a psychologist and the reason for her visit.

Picking up the common thread between the establishment where she was practicing, the school director's request, and the mother's reply, I asked the student what having a place meant to her. She told me she was her parents' favorite daughter. This had put her in a painful situation with respect to her siblings, so in her eyes having a place meant stealing it from others.

It then occurred to me that this supervision which I had begun was going to have to be continued from the next session by one of my colleagues, so in the training group as well everything happened as if places were interchangeable. Here too one could say that everything was arranged so that it was impossible to establish a specific relationship between the student and the supervisor.

If I Count for You, Don't Let Me Count

The couple in this case had come to consult at a hospital where I was supervising a team of family therapists. One therapist interviewed the couple while the other team members and myself observed through a one-way mirror.

The husband was a professional, the wife was newly self-employed. Both of them complained of constant marital conflict. In the first session these patients said to the psychiatrist who was seeing them that they would have preferred to see me in my private office but that they hadn't contacted me because they assumed that my fee was too high for them. They had decided to come to the hospital, knowing that the therapy was under my supervision. Then, even while talking constantly about money and financial conflicts, they described how little they had counted for their families of origin and how little, currently, each counted for the other. Each of them wanted to count for the other, but didn't believe that this was possible.

After several sessions, an urgent problem called me away from the hospital just as they were waiting to be seen. As I took a corridor that ran past the waiting room, they saw me leave. At the beginning of the session the husband told the therapist that they had expected the meeting would be canceled and the wife added, "I don't count. Doctor Elkaïm has left." After they alluded many times to a possible separation. They emphasized that this outcome seemed unavoidable, but they didn't see how they could separate. The longer the session went on, the more the therapist and the team members behind the one-way mirror felt that the link between separation and not counting could have a creative side. During the session break they prepared the following intervention.

Each member of the couple, said the therapist, wants to count. At the same time they assert that they have never had a positive experience in this area, that they don't believe they can ever count for someone, and that they are convinced that if in some extraordinary way such a situation arose it could lead only to a betrayal. So perhaps to some extent each one imagines that it is terribly important to help the other avoid having to come to grips with this belief. As long as each one can complain that the other isn't allowing him or her to count, they can avoid having to ask if they would be able to accept being able to count at last without becoming terrified.

The therapist went on to say that when they took the role of intimate enemy with each other she saw them as playing the masked defender, attracting hostile attention to spare the other from fears that would otherwise be even crueler.

When I got back I was struck by the ease with which the therapist, helped by the rest of the team, had carried out this positive reframing of the complaints the spouses were making to each other and had accompanied it with an extremely interesting paradoxical commentary. I was all the more surprised because this psychiatrist, who was a remarkable therapist with an analytic orientation and who had trained with me in the systemic approach, was generally quite resistant to this type of intervention.

When we discussed the session, it turned out that the therapist and the other team members had all, for very different reasons, strongly experienced the sensation of not counting at one or another moment of their lives. And we also found out that, as the result of my sudden departure, certain of them had had the feeling that they didn't count enough in my eyes.

The members of the couple were asking us to show them that they counted without being able to believe that they could. Faced with this double bind we had inadvertently addressed both these levels at the same time. The therapist, by seeing them, had clearly shown them how much they did count, while I, by leaving, had helped them not to fear that in the end they could count for someone.

This common thread connecting the couple and the members of the therapy team extended also to our setting, because these family therapy consultations were only just beginning and they still counted for very little in the university hospital where they were taking place.

Resonances

Resonances are those special assemblages created by the intersection of different systems that include the same element.
Different human systems seem to enter into resonance from
the effect of a common element in the same way that material
bodies can begin to vibrate from the effect of a given frequency.

Resonances and Self-reference

These resonances do not exist in themselves. They arise in
couplings, in the intersections of the constructions of reality
of the members of the system. Resonance is not an "objective
fact." It is not a hidden truth that can be shown by pointing
to a common intersection between different systems. It is born
in the interaction between the person who is describing the
resonance and the context in its complexity.

The Threshold Effect

You will notice, in the situations described above, that there
is a triggering incident, a sort of falling into place that occurs
at a certain point. For example, in the second situation above,
"Being There and Not Being There," when the therapist
showed her irritation, something happened between her and
me which was like a threshold; after that the resonance could
come into being. And in the situation entitled "Having a
Place," what I experienced before a young student whose hair
hid an attractive face shows us the same thing: abruptly, seemingly trivial elements came together and a whole new field of
possibilities appeared.

Resonance and Intervention

How can we use this concept of resonance? It seems that work done on a given point of resonance with a given protagonist of a specific system changes the other systems that are in interrelationship with it. This is how an important change took place in the therapeutic system of the father whose son had been labeled as psychotic since the age of ten, following work that I did in supervision with the therapist. The father-son dyad became less symbiotic, the son stopped making his stereotyped gestures and constantly protecting his father against all external intrusions, and the father and son began to talk about their isolation. Moreover, when the therapist arrived late one day, the son was able to talk about his fear that his father and he were not important enough for her.

I do not propose to undertake an exhaustive academic study of resonating systems—the ones that I have been able to describe or those that other practitioners have spotted—but rather to consider what we have to deal with in clinical applications.

For purely practical reasons, when we are working with supervision groups, the resonating systems we focus on most often are the family system of the patient, the therapist's family of origin, the institutional system, and the supervision group. We try to work with the points of intersection between the different systems that are operating in order to change the systems in resonance.

It is obvious that the intervention depends on the setting where the therapist works. If the setting is in an institution, a priority can be given to changing the resonance there. But other systems can play an important role in resonance. For example, I once supervised a team of South American women psychologists who were using my approach with multifamily groups (Elkaïm, 1979, 1980a). They asked me to work on the case of some single mothers who had problem children. Some of the fathers of these children had disappeared during the period of military dictatorship that their country had recently experienced. The director of the place where these psychologists practiced had told them that they were "underground therapists." They had no fixed place for holding their multifamily sessions and very few of them were being paid. Many points of resonance appeared in the supervision system—disappearance, clandestineness, violence, not having a place, and so forth—but I worked only with the particular point of resonance that was closest to me and that seemed to involve all of the members of the therapeutic team.

The positive change in the families and the subsequent improvement in the status of the team members in their institution does not mean that I was "right" to choose a particular point of resonance. Perhaps the work done around a specific theme common to the different interrelated systems simply enlarged the field of what was possible.

Social Context, Resonance, and Homeostasis

The initial context for my practice of family therapy was social psychiatry. Having first worked in the South Bronx in New York City and then in a poor district in Brussels, I had from the beginning the good luck to see that it is very difficult to deal with a mental health problem without relating it not only to family factors but also to social, cultural, and political factors (Elkaïm, 1977, 1987). I therefore developed multifamily therapies that were different from the ones that existed at the time. Contrary to what was then recommended, I met with families that had the same type of problem and were living in the same socioeconomic context, which allowed me to get a glimpse of how an apparently individual problem could also be a collective problem. And

I also transformed the network interventions of Ross Speck and Carolyn Attneave (1973) into what at the time I called network practices. In this approach, the members of the enlarged system could see the problem of an individual as the problem of a group caught in the same social and political contradictions.

At that time, my construction of reality was very meager. I saw the world more or less as a set of Russian dolls nested one inside the other. I started with the individual, went on to the family, then to the neighborhood, to the social context, and so on. More recently, the concept of resonance has allowed me to see that these different systems can be joined by a link that is more than the quasi-mechanical replication of the same rule from one level to the next.

But the concept of resonance raises another question: Can we still think in terms of homeostasis when the systems that are resonating together are so different? In a pinch, when the systems involved are the family systems of the therapist and the patient and the institutional system of the place where the family is being seen, we can still think in terms of a rule that is common to different interrelated systems and necessary to their homeostasis. But when these systems are also social and political, as in the case of the multifamily therapy I have just been referring to, can we continue to think in terms of strict homeostasis?

Let us go back to the example of Bianca in chapter 4. The word *chosen* reminds me of a whole series of ideas, including the notion of the Chosen People, Chaim Potok's novel *The Chosen,* and the view of my old philosophy professor Emmanuel Levinas that the Jews were chosen not as a privilege but as a duty. How can we integrate these resonating elements with the concept of homeostasis in a strict sense? I don't have an answer to this question, but it seems important for me to ask it.

Resonance, Meaning, and Function

When it comes to the concepts of meaning and function, we can ask the same question that we have asked about homeostasis. It is natural to understand a context in terms of meaning and function when the systems involved form a coherent relationship, but can we still think in these terms when the resonance brings into play domains that are so separate as to be completely outside of the classical understanding of what a system is?

Assemblages

General Laws, Intrinsic Rules, and Singularities

What is the connection between the concept of resonance and the concept of assemblages presented in chapter 2? Let me review what I mean by *assemblage*. I give the name to the whole created by interrelated elements interacting in a given situation. These can be genetic or biological elements as well as ones linked to family rules or aspects of society or culture. A therapeutic assemblage can be made up of elements to which general laws apply, of elements linked to the intrinsic rules that belong to that particular therapeutic system, and also of singularities, which can be either significant or "nonsignificant."

Resonance is simply a particular kind of assemblage made up of the intersection of different systems around the same element. Resonances are the redundancies that connect the most dissimilar universes, while singularities, even if they are self-referential, remain unique.

In the case of the North African Jewish family described in chapter 2, we saw the working of laws that apply to different open systems, like homeostasis, as well as intrinsic rules like those that allowed us to understand the functions of these patients' symptoms. In addition, a series of singularities were set in motion—water, perspiring, tears, the use of space, a way of speaking. These elements were self-referential and involved all the members of the therapeutic system. Certain of them lead us to different elements but could also take us back just to themselves. Singularities that play a role in and of themselves I call nonsignificant singularities.

I have the impression that singularities, although they are often thought of as more or less irrelevant, as the slag of the therapeutic process, nevertheless frequently play the role of a catalyst for the development of that therapeutic process.

During a recent conference in the United States, Peter Sifneos, a specialist in brief therapy, told the following story: one of his patients told him she did not think the content of what he said to her in the sessions did her much good, but all she had to do was to remember the sound of his accent to get much better. This accent could evoke a whole chain of significant elements, but couldn't we imagine that it also played a role in and of itself?

In the example of the North African family, couldn't the water have a life of its own, above and beyond the metaphoric and other aspects to which it refers? And can we speak of the aesthetic shock produced by seeing a picture or hearing a piece of music simply in terms of meaning or function? Isn't this to reduce the underlying richness of what we experience?

The Observer's Participation in the System

The second cybernetics of Heinz von Foerster is concerned with feedbacks not only among the members of the observed system (which is what the first cybernetics were all about) but also above all between the observing system and the observed system. Both von Foerster and Varela emphasize that the observer cannot be separated from what is observed, because the observer participates in the very system he or she is observing.

How does the observer emerge as observer in the system? How do his or her thoughts come about? To what extent is the observer free with respect to the system? How can new things arise in the system? These questions remain open. In raising the concepts of resonance and assemblage in these pages, I have simply wanted to contribute to a rough outline of an answer. These concepts do have the advantage of leaving the door open to explanations of every sort, and thus avoiding having the question of the observer's emergence confined in the straitjacket of a one-dimensional reading. As far as change is concerned, what determines the development of a system will be more connected to the way in which the intervener gets involved in order to allow various elements to interact than to any discovery of a hidden truth.

In some cultural contexts, of course, going through a stage where the intersections of reality are built around the discovery of hidden truths may be an indispensable step in the construction of a fruitful assemblage. The discovery of hidden truths will then be one of the necessary components of that assemblage.

It seems to me that writers like Proust are masters of the art of creating descriptions that leave open many ways of looking at things and rule out simplistic understandings. Commenting on the passage in *Remembrance of Things Past* where Swann associates Odette's face with Botticelli's portrait of Zipporah in a Sistine Chapel fresco, Félix Guattari (1979) writes:

What is the origin of the devastating power of Odette's face? . . . Isn't it a question of a "regressive identification" on the part of Swann with a maternal figure, of a deficit in him of a symbolic paternal side which could allow him to "accept his castration" in an appropriate way? After all, wasn't Zipporah, whose face is superimposed over Odette's, given to Moses by his father, the priest Jethro, as a token of his return to the God of Abraham? And wasn't that fresco in the Sistine Chapel conceived as a counterpoint between the life of Moses and the life of Jesus? Doesn't that show us that we are involved with a parallel between Swann's archaic fixation on an *imaginary* equivalent of the evil, incestuous mother/whore/daughter and an essentially *symbolic* Christian vision of an original lack of the paternal function? Besides, isn't it following his marriage with Odette and the sublimation of his incestuous passion that, on the occasion of the Dreyfus affair, Swann finally comes to the point of acknowledging his Jewishness? (P. 246)

Guattari shows here that one can force the details described by Proust into the framework of traditional psychoanalytic interpretation, but goes on to point out that then one bypasses the singularity of Odette's face, the theme of Vinteuil's musical phrase, the disposition of the Verdurins' salon, other universes, other becomings. A reductionist reading that would impose its understanding on artistic creation or on psychotherapy ignores the fact that elements which are seemingly unimportant in certain conditions can become determining when these conditions change. From this point of view, psychotherapy can be defined as the art of keeping the possible possible.

7
"Thinking with the Feet": Intervention in Family Therapy

ONE spring day in Marrakech, while my mother and I were on a walk, we came across our maid. My mother asked the woman where she was going; she replied, "Wherever my feet lead me." Being only a child, I didn't see her answer as an attempt to sidestep the question. Thinking that it had to have some meaning, I asked myself how feet could think. The problem had me deeply perplexed.

Many years later I began to get a glimpse of the relevance of this thought, in the course of an intervention that occurred during a family therapy supervision. I have already described that family in chapter 1. The members of the family were afflicted with many health problems and the mother and her two daughters came into the room on crutches. We had developed the hypothesis that we were involved with a family for which helping was an important rule, but in which at the same time there was never any question of asking for help from anyone else. We saw in this contradiction the double bind "Help us," but "We can only give help; we can't accept it."

After discussing the situation with the supervision group, the therapist wanted to reframe the family members' symptoms as a way of inviting help without having to ask for it. By emphasizing that a physical problem allowed the other person to rush to the aid of the one who was sick, this interpretation reframed the symptoms positively. At the same time the reframing was accompanied by a paradoxical implication, since it suggested that the help that was being so disparaged was nevertheless perhaps being implicitly requested. The therapist hoped that the interpretation would lead the members of the family to give up the symptoms she had reframed in this way. She hoped that they would then dare to explore richer and less dangerous possibilities.

Just before leaving the supervision room, the therapist tripped on the rug and restored her balance by supporting herself against the wall. Back in the therapy room, her intervention, which we followed on closed-circuit television, rather quickly ground to a halt. Obviously, the therapist was not succeeding in her attempt to show that she could help, and at the same time she wasn't able to use the difficulties that she was experiencing as a therapeutic tool. In those days I would still sometimes go into the therapy room in my role of consultant when a student was having trouble,* which is what I did in this case. Here is the beginning of my intervention:

MONY ELKAÏM [*Coming into the therapy room and greeting the different family members one after another*]: Hello, everybody. Forgive me for interrupting you. [*To the mother*]: Hello, madame. [*To the elder daughter*]: Hello. [*To the younger daughter*]: Hello. [*To the father*]: Hello, monsieur.

---

*Nowadays, except in very rare cases, I intervene only from behind the one-way mirror. What counts for me, indeed, is to work on the intersections between the constructions of reality of my student and the members of the family, relying on the self-referential aspect of my own experience. It seems to me that remaining behind the one-way mirror shows more respect for the special bridge that exists between the family and the therapist and gives the therapist the chance to come up with his or her own intervention. When the consultation takes place in the therapy room, it is necessary to take into account, in addition to these elements, the coupling between the consultant's singularities and those of the other members of the therapeutic system.

Suddenly, even as I was shaking hands with the father, I tangled my foot in the wire of the microphone and almost fell. I avoided going down only by grabbing the hand the father was holding out to me.

M.E. [*To the father*]: Thank you for helping me.

Then I took a place between the father and the therapist. We were sitting in a circle—the mother, the two daughters, the father, myself, and the therapist.

FATHER: Was that a setup? Did you plan to do that?
M.E.: No, I certainly didn't plan to tangle my foot in the microphone wire, but maybe that's what happens in this family. [*The mother laughs.*] Perhaps I'm showing a white paw.* [*I hold out my right hand, palm toward the family. The mother, smiling, holds out her hand, which is wrapped in a bandage, a very white bandage.*] And how can I show the white paw except by asking you to help me when I myself have come to help you?

My feet had just found a solution to the double bind. In addition, they had allowed me to put in action the intervention that my student had prepared, that is, getting helped in order to help.

---

*This is referring to a French nursery story. A mother sheep has to leave her lambs alone in their house. "There are dangerous animals out there," she warns. "If anyone knocks, don't let them in unless the foot they knock with is white like a sheep's." A clever wolf overhears the warning. He dips his paw in flour before he knocks . . .

"Showing the white paw" means "giving the password" in French, but there is a suggestion of danger.

Hypotheses, Creativity, and the Therapeutic System

Is it necessary to state that my fall was in no way premeditated? The fact that it could be understood as a solution to the family's double bind arose from the context of the hypothesis that we had developed. Without a doubt, the hypothesis had to be in place for this act of creativity which led to the establishment of a new therapeutic system to occur.

This brief example poses the problem of how creative acts come about in therapy. If I had planned what I did, it would have lost all its impact, because no "setup," to use the father's language, could manifest the spontaneity and force of the sudden creative act. Besides, it is often when the therapist is totally stuck that something suddenly wells up from nowhere and afterward seems to have played a crucial role in unblocking the therapeutic system. The following is a case that seems to me to be a particularly illuminating example.

The case involved a touching twenty-seven-year-old patient who had been anorexic, with bulimic episodes, since the age of fourteen. Accustomed to taking huge doses of laxatives and diuretics, this young woman was addicted to several medications. She had attempted suicide on many occasions and had had multiple hospitalizations. I followed her for three years in family therapy while she was being seen in individual therapy by a fellow psychiatrist.

In spite of all my efforts, and even though I thought I had pretty well understood the factors that were maintaining the patient's symptoms, the therapeutic results were minimal. In the course of the third year of treatment, I decided that it was impossible to keep on calmly seeing this cooperative family while the life of the patient was in danger and while my interventions were turning out to be so ineffective. I therefore told the family that I had failed and that the situation was too serious for me to continue as if nothing was wrong. I proposed that I be supervised by some former students who had become my colleagues and asked the family to stop seeing me in my private office and to come instead to the institute where my colleagues were working. In the weeks that followed, the therapy took place in the institute, under the supervision of my colleagues.

This episode seems to have been the key moment in the therapy. The patient's condition got progressively better and she met a man with whom she became seriously involved. I saw them together for a limited number of sessions (the man had some problems himself), and then my patient and her friend moved to another country. A year later, the young woman wrote me to say that she was doing very well and was no longer having eating problems or taking too much medication. She told me she was eager to have a baby, and the next year I got a card announcing the blessed event.

Perhaps it is only in my eyes that the episode played an essential role. It may be that something especially important happened in the patient's individual therapy at that moment—she had an excellent relationship with her individual therapist. It is also possible that her gaining a husband and their forming a new couple profoundly altered the rules of the systems she had grown up in. . . . It is certain that all these elements, together, played a role that cannot be underestimated. Nevertheless, what happened in the family therapy seems at least as crucial to me.

Therapists dealing with anorexia are very familiar with the power struggle that generally takes place between the patient and those around her. They are not unfamiliar with the feeling of powerlessness that grips the therapist confronted with a patient who seems to bring people to their knees by turning her aggression on herself. Even so, I didn't construct my intervention in order to underline the futility of the power struggle. I wasn't trying to show that I, like the parents, could fail and nevertheless accept help (in my case from colleagues who were younger than me) in order to get out of my impasse. The creative act arose as a spontaneous reaction to my awareness of failure, and if it encouraged the appearance of new possibilities, it was perhaps because of its spontaneity.

Jean-Luc Giribone (1988) points out the dilemma. He describes the creative act that completely changes a situation as an act "which would change its nature, would lose its effectiveness, would even cease to exist as a creative act, if it were performed with the conscious goal of achieving the result which it can only achieve by not making it the goal." In order to escape this difficulty, Giribone quotes the words of the Yaqui sorcerer Don Juan, as reported by his apprentice Carlos Castaneda (1972) in *Journey to Ixtlan*. Teaching Castaneda the art of being a warrior, Don Juan says: "A warrior . . . is a hunter. He calculates everything. That's control. But once his calculations are over, he acts. He lets go. That's abandon" (p. 150). Giribone says we should thus distinguish two separate processes. The preparation of the creative act and the act itself, he writes, should occur at two distinct times, first the one and then the other.

I am not convinced that such a separation is always possible in our field. Another case where I tripped and slipped—this time on my own tongue, not on a microphone wire—will show what I mean. About ten minutes before the end of a group supervisory session, a student asked if it would be all right to talk about a personal problem: she wondered if she was capable of being a psychotherapist. At the beginning of the last year of training in another professional field her professor had warned the class that not everyone would get through the year and graduate. Although she had never failed any of her courses, she took these comments as addressed to her and decided to drop out of the program and go to social work school. Now she was feeling the same doubts about becoming a psychotherapist.

I felt that I was confronted by a double bind. I hypothesized that her official program was "I want to succeed," while her construction of the world was "I cannot succeed." If, as her trainer, I responded to only one of the two levels, I would run into the other. If I wanted to get her unstuck, my intervention would have to respond to both levels at once.

But I felt that before I could intervene I needed to verify my hypothesis. In Don Juan's terms, I needed to calculate before I acted. However, in this particular situation, I surprised myself by asking the student if she had a husband who was making a good living. Yes. Children? Yes. Then I said I was puzzled: I couldn't understand why she had to pursue a career when she could stay home and take care of her husband and children. "You sound just like my father," she replied. "He's always saying that I don't need a career: I should just be a good wife and mother." At this point in the discussion, I found myself in a situation where, at the same time, I verified my hypothesis and responded to both levels of the double bind in which she was caught up. On the one hand, the training context and the fact that she was my student implied a contract of assistance. This placed me in the role of someone who was trying to help her succeed. I thus met her official program. On the other hand, my telling her to give up her career allowed me to respond to her construction of the world. At the same time, my pompous and exaggerated position perplexed her in such a way that she did not know whether I really meant what I said or not.

This tongue-in-cheek aspect, when accompanied by a certain warmth, is crucial to this kind of approach. It is similar to the technique described by Carl Whitaker (1975) when he speaks of making the Tower of Pisa higher and higher until it finally crumbles on its own. It seems to me that the psychotherapist who magnifies the dysfunctional rules of a system, or one who exaggerates the patient's fears, is performing more than an amplification: he or she is maneuvering in a therapeutic context that is implicitly bound to a contract of assistance. This allies the therapist to the official program of the patient. The provocative aspect of the intervention allows the therapist, at the same time, to respond to the construction of the world of that person without being engulfed by it. The therapist thus succeeds in being simultaneously on both of the double bind's levels.

Then I began embroidering my theme. I said I didn't see any harm in protecting her father: nowadays all too many young people do exactly the opposite. What was remarkable was the fact that while the members of the group disagreed with what I was saying, the student stood up for me, insisting that what I had just said was exactly what she herself thought. At that moment, I made a slip of the tongue. Instead of saying, "What's wrong with protecting your father?" I said, "What's wrong with protecting your husband?" "My husband?" she shot back. "Never!" Then she became thoughtful and said that when her husband's father was the age her husband now was, he had become depressed and unable to work and her husband's mother had to go to work to support the family. As a result of this unplanned intervention, she not only experienced the dilemma of her double bind in a different way but also began to see herself as protecting her husband and the rules of her family of origin simultaneously. She later told me that a few weeks later, from the delayed impact of this interaction, she surprised herself by suddenly becoming very creative in a difficult case and from then on she never experienced what she called her "hesitation waltz."

It will be seen that when I thought I was at the stage of exploring intrinsic rules by my hypothesis testing I was already in the sway of the system's singularities. My slip certainly arose from an assemblage of singularities associated with the training group, the student, and myself. But I want to emphasize that it is not always possible to separate the preparation and the creative act of intervention.

In spite of this, systemic therapists and supervisors place

their emphasis on the work of preparation. As for creativity, it can come only as an extra, a sort of crowning of the work. Degas's portrait of Mme. Théodore Gobillard, née Morisot, which was painted in 1869 and now hangs in the Metropolitan Museum in New York, illustrates wonderfully the connection between preparation and spontaneity. The oil painting was preceded by many studies, some showing Mme. Gobillard without a background, some showing the room she was in without any figure. Clearly Degas spent a long time preparing the work, but this premeditation doesn't in the least take away from the remarkable spontaneity of the final portrait.

The development of hypotheses is a fundamental stage in therapy. For me, it consists not of finding hidden rules but rather of a joint construction by the therapist and the members of the family. It is a joint invention, surprising and yet plausible. The most important moment in the first session is the one during which the hypothesis is constructed. The family members move step by step into the explanatory framework that the therapist has adopted in his or her inquiry, while at the same time bringing the therapist into their constructions of reality. The hypothesis cannot be fruitfully shared by the members of the therapeutic system unless it is both close enough to be acceptable and surprising enough to justify a new understanding. In my opinion it is during this hypothesis development phase that the therapeutic system is formed and that the foundations of a new, shared vision of the world are laid. The moment at the end of the session when the hypothesis is used is only a commentary; the essential game has already been played. Naturally the systemic therapist does not stop with suggesting hypotheses or redefining situations. He or she suggests homework tasks. But these tasks will have an impact only if the different members of the therapeutic system share in the construction of the framework of meaning on which they are based. If the therapeutic intervention succeeds, the shared hypothesis has become a meaningful basis for action.

Experiencing the Same Situation Differently

It is not enough, however, to share the same hypothesis. In the case of the family mentioned above, the therapist also told me that she had developed a violent backache. The pains had come on at the end of a session in which the mother had mentioned that she knew several excellent physical therapists and offered her their addresses in case she ever needed them. The backache didn't get better until after the fall I described and the intervention that followed.

So a new intersection was created between the reality constructions of the therapist and the family members and a new system appeared; but for all that, the system had not become therapeutic. The therapeutic alliance is always necessary, but sometimes it is not enough. In order for a hypothesis to lead to a successful intervention, it must not only surprise people but also allow them to experience the same situation differently.

Understanding Differently versus Disqualifying the Patient

The search for a different understanding must not make us deaf to what our patients are saying. Too often, systemic therapists are so absorbed in trying to understand the presenting symptom in a circular way that they forget to take into account the feelings of disqualification that the person they are talking to may be experiencing.

To take an example, let us imagine an adolescent who lashes out viciously at his parents, and let us also imagine that the therapist is content to reframe the young man's anger as a way of turning his parents' attention on himself and distracting them from their conflict with each other. There is a good chance that the adolescent will see the therapist as unable to accept his aggressiveness and as rejecting anything that doesn't fit the therapist's own vision of the world.

When I say that a hypothesis should be surprising, I do not mean it should reject the many alternative ways of constructing the universe that the members of the system may have. The joint construction that they realize with the help of the therapist should be offered as one supplementary possibility and not as a truth that rules out all other possible understandings of reality.

Seeing That You Do Not See

A situation described by Heinz von Foerster (1984b) shows the importance of seeking out supplementary possibilities. Sometimes when a soldier has received a bullet wound in the occipital region of the brain, the wound heals fairly quickly but after a few weeks motor disturbances begin to appear— for example, in an arm or a leg. Clinical tests show that the functioning of the nerves controlling the motor system is normal but that a substantial part of the visual field has been destroyed, a loss of which the patient has absolutely no awareness. "A successful therapy consists of blind-folding the patient over a period of one or two months until he gains control over his motor system by shifting his 'attention' from (nonexistent) visual cues regarding his posture to (fully operative) channels that give direct postural clues from (proprioceptive) sensors embedded in muscles and joints" (p. 43).

The patient doesn't see that he doesn't see, and, not seeing it, is unable to explore new possibilities or find a solution to the problem. It is only when he starts seeing it that a new development can arise. In this sense therapy can be viewed as a process of helping people to see that they don't see, and to work on this very limitation in order to open up new possibilities for themselves.

Constraint and Autonomy

This connection between limitation and possibility, between constraint and autonomy, brings us back to the question of what freedom observers have with respect to the contexts in which they find themselves, of what autonomy the therapist or the patient has with respect to the systems that they are members of.

Not all limitations are constraints that we can escape. Old age, death, the inherent shortcomings of our human condition, are fundamental aspects of our destiny. Among the many available ways of coping with our limitations, I want to mention two that have particularly struck me.

First, I have always been moved by the drama of Sisyphus. Listen to Homer:

> *Then Sisyphus in torment I beheld*
> *being roustabout to a tremendous boulder.*
> *Leaning with both arms braced and legs driving,*
> *he heaved it toward a height, and almost over,*
> *but then a Power spun him round and sent*
> *the cruel boulder bounding down again to the plain.*
> *Whereupon the man bent down again to toil,*
> *dripping sweat, and the dust rose overhead.*

The judges of Hades had condemned Sisyphus to push a huge boulder to the top of a hill in order to send it down the slope on the other side. But scarcely would Sisyphus arrive at the top when the rock would throw him back and then hurtle down, carried by its own weight.

We can say at the least that Sisyphus was a particularly wily man. When Autolycus tried to steal his cattle, Sisyphus was able to thwart his plan in spite of the fact that Hermes had given the thief the power to change the form of the animals whenever he wanted to. And when Zeus sent Death, the brother of Sleep, to take him to Tartary and subject him to eternal punishment for having betrayed the secrets of the gods, Sisyphus was able to take Death by surprise and fetter him in chains.

With Death being a prisoner, people were no longer able to die. To escape this impasse, Ares freed Death and turned Sisyphus over to him. But Sisyphus still had not run out of ideas. He instructed his wife, Merope, not to bury him, so that when he got to the palace of Hades he was able to ask Persephone for permission to return to earth to get buried and to punish those who had not performed their funerary duties. Persephone sent him back to earth for three days, which allowed him to escape once more.

Hermes had to catch him and bring him by force back to Hades. What could Sisyphus do now to extricate himself from the affair? Albert Camus (1955), in *The Myth of Sisyphus,* gives him the final victory:

Then Sisyphus watches the stone rush down in a few moments toward the lower world whence he will have to push it up again toward the summit. He goes back down to the plain.

It is during that return, that pause, that Sisyphus interests me. . . . Sisyphus, proletarian of the gods, powerless and rebellious, knows the whole extent of his wretched condition: it is what he thinks of during his descent. The lucidity of what was to constitute his torture at the same time crowns his victory.

For Camus, it is when Sisyphus rejects the gods, when he makes fate the concern of humans, that he takes charge of his fate and makes the rock his own. From the outside, Sisyphus may appear to be a condemned man, repeating for eternity the same useless actions, but for him this boulder is his boulder and this hopeless enterprise is his enterprise—it is no longer imposed on him, he lays claim to it. Let the rock continue to tumble: whatever the verdict of the gods, Sisyphus is his own master. His halo is not the halo of the martyr who has achieved sainthood; perhaps his only halo is the "dust overhead," but it is this dust, this boulder, his human condition, which constitute his grandeur.

In a livelier key, Charles Perrault (1972), in his fairy tale *Sleeping Beauty,* also tries to integrate a limitation in order to escape its slavery. Recall the story. The old fairy who was not invited to the baptismal ceremony has just condemned the princess to die from piercing her finger with a spindle. The young fairy emerges from the place where she has been hiding in order to give her gift last and declares: "Take comfort, King and Queen, your daughter will not die. It is true that I am not powerful enough to undo all that the old fairy has done. The Princess will prick her hand with a spindle, but, instead of dying from it, she will fall into a deep sleep that will last a hundred years. At the end of that time a King's son will come to wake her up."

I often think that, like Sisyphus and the young fairy, we cannot avoid coming to terms with our human condition and the context in which we find ourselves. Like them, we cannot erase what has happened; we can only try to transform our handicaps into advantages. For this to occur, however, the systems we are part of must be open to change.

In the Land of the Blind, the One-Eyed Person . . .

One day, during a workshop we were co-leading, Heinz von Foerster mentioned a little-known aspect of Plato's allegory of the cave. In Book 7 of *The Republic,* Socrates imagines a cave whose mouth is open to the light. Some men have lived there since childhood, manacled in such a way that they can see only the wall at the back of their prison. Light comes from a fire burning on an elevation far behind them. Between the fire and the prisoners there runs a road bordered by a small wall. People walk behind this wall carrying all kinds of objects and figures of men and animals; these project above the wall. All the captives can see are the shadows of these things thrown by the firelight on the wall at the back of the cave, and all they can hear are the echoes of the voices of the people behind the wall.

If one of the prisoners were freed from his chains and brought outside, it would take him some time to get used to the light and the outside world. And if by chance he came back to the place where he had grown up and tried to convince his former companions of the existence of an external reality, he would run up against their total disbelief. He would even run the risk of being killed if he persisted in trying to free them and lead them out of their prison. Commenting on this, von Foerster said, "In the land of the blind, the one-eyed person ends up in the mental hospital!"

I quote von Foerster not to contrast the world of darkness and the world of light or, as Socrates would say, the world of ignorance and the world of knowledge, but rather to emphasize the importance of the system in which change arises. In order for a change to be able to amplify and spread, in order for every variation not to be brought back to some preexisting norm, certain conditions have to be met. For an intervention to modify a human system over the long term, it is necessary that the change affect the way every one of the members of the system sees things. And that change can be brought about in many ways.

Some Principles Underlying My Therapeutic Approach

Toward a Systemic Sense of Time

It is important in therapy to go beyond a simplistic choice between a view of history according to which elements of the past automatically determine elements of the future and an interpretation in the name of systemic equifinality that attends only to the here and now. Family therapies need to approach time more flexibly than this. Elements of the past generally turn out to be necessary but not sufficient for an understanding of the present. In order for a past traumatic event to keep on having a role in the present, it is necessary that the continuance of a behavior have an important function and meaning in the system where it is being perpetuated. We can see a good example of this when a couple gets together.

Let us imagine a woman who, for reasons connected to her history, is not happy in a couple relationship unless she is in the role of the comforter. Let us suppose that their first few times together, each time her partner is silent or seems lost in thought she imagines he is sad. And let us finally imagine that she asks him, "Are you sad?" letting him know how willing she is to be close to him and help him if he says yes. If her partner decides to respond to her implicit invitation, the couple system will amplify and maintain these behaviors, which are linked to past events. But we could also imagine that he would answer, "No, I'm not sad. I'm just thinking of something." She certainly might stop seeing him, but if she stays with him anyway, this particular aspect of her personality may well end up not being amplified and maintained.

After all, the same thing is supposed to happen in individual dynamic therapy. The patient tries to reenact with the therapist earlier relationships, but the therapist, by his or her reaction, creates a different context which will, when the time is ripe, allow the patient to try out new behaviors.

In addition, time as I understand it, in the light of the writings of the chemist Ilya Prigogine and his group, is no longer a linear time in which the elements succeed each other in an orderly process of cause and effect. The amplification of certain assemblages, in which chance certainly plays a part, can effectively lead to an abrupt transition, a bifurcation, a new and unforeseen becoming.

Assemblages and Self-reference

In chapter 2, I made a major point of the self-referential assemblages that had appeared during a therapy session. These assemblages, formed of both intrinsic rules and singularities, can become amplified at a given moment and assume a consistency that changes the development of the therapeutic system. The assemblage that can block or encourage the evolution of the therapeutic system is formed from elements linked to different members of the therapeutic system but not reducible to them. The art of the therapist consists of going with the family's flow in order to allow these assemblages to form, even if they do not correspond exactly with what is supposed to be important in the therapist's explanatory framework.

These assemblages belong not only to the family system but also to the therapeutic system. The therapist is always included. It is essential, it seems to me, that the therapist not try to know what is good for the family or to decide what direction the therapeutic system ought to take. The work should consist rather of helping the family members to not follow relationship patterns that keep the symptom going, in order to open up other possibilities. As for these possibilities, the therapist discovers them at the same time as the family members; and the therapist also changes to the extent that he or she helps the family members change. Therapy can be described as a succession of situations in which the therapist tries to help the therapeutic system get out of the rut it is stuck in.

A Systemic View of Feelings

The first tool in therapy is the therapist's own self. For a long time therapists distrusted the feelings that patients evoked in them because they thought that their affect could only taint the "objectivity" of their observations. I personally am not convinced that what we experience as therapists when we are doing psychotherapy is a handicap. Naturally, we cannot experience a particular feeling unless the specific situation touches some string in us. But for me, the meaning and function of the string's vibration should not be sought only in my own dynamics: they are also connected to the system where I am experiencing the feeling. To put it differently, in the same way that for the systemic therapist the identified patient's symptom has a meaning and a function in the family system, I hold that the feelings that arise in any member of a therapeutic system have a meaning and function with respect to that therapeutic system. For me, these feelings mark the specific bridges that are being built between the family members and the therapist. They establish the common foundations on which the therapy can be erected.

I do not mean that therapists can ignore the risk that their personal feelings create—far from it. Only an acute awareness of these risks will allow therapists to avoid confirming the world views of the members of the family as well as their own. And there are certainly times when feelings that are too invasive can lead therapists to reinforce in the family members the feelings they are trying to understand. But even this situation cannot continue unless it has a function in relation to the whole therapeutic system. (In the last section of this chapter, I will show how the therapist can use self-reference in the session as an asset rather than a handicap.)

Resonances

It seems to me essential, during therapy or supervision, not to lose sight of the different systems involved. The search for points of resonance can turn out to be crucial for the development of the therapeutic system.

Some Tools for Intervention

In this section I return to the notion of reframing, a tool used by all the schools of systemic therapy, then present a type of intervention I have developed in couple therapy, and finally describe how self-reference can become a trump card in the hands of the systemic therapist.

Reframing

I have already talked about reframing in chapter 2. Recall that Watzlawick, Weakland, and Fisch (1974) say that reframing consists of modifying the context of a situation in order to completely change its meaning. At this point I cannot resist the pleasure of mentioning a case that Françoise Dolto described on French television. She was seeing a mother who was anxious because even though she had gone through the pregnancy very well her newborn infant was refusing her milk; unfortunately, he took the bottles the nurse gave him without any problem. Dolto explained to the mother, who was feeling very bad about the situation, that her child loved her so much he wanted to love her in the same way he had in the womb, when he didn't yet have a mouth. This intervention completely changed the mother's relationship with the baby, and with the nurse who was feeding him.

The underlying richness of this reframing springs immediately to our eyes. Among other things, it emphasizes that the infant as well as the mother misses the wonderful period that the pregnancy had been, suggesting that the mother isn't the only person who feels nostalgia for it. Undoubtedly other factors, which I haven't picked up on, also played a role. For example, why did Dolto say that the fetus didn't have a mouth rather than saying it didn't take nourishment through its mouth? These details are part of the extremely complex constellation that surrounds every therapeutic intervention. The actual assemblage is always a lot richer than the rationalized description we are able to give of it.

Reframing is one of the tools that systemic therapists use the most. To go back to the family that I talked about at the beginning of this chapter, for example, in the course of the same session the mother complained that she was "a gourd,"* meaning that she was stupid. Later in the therapy the consultant took the word and used it in another meaning, a container that can be used to quench your thirst in the desert. Can't we imagine that it was precisely by acting like "a gourd" in the family's meaning of the word that the mother enabled the others to quench their thirst?

In order for reframings to be accepted, they have to be culturally plausible to the people who hear them. In our field family members are often described as "protecting each other" or the presenting symptom as seeming to protect the family members in the eyes of the identified patient. The success of this particular reframing may arise from the fact

*In French the word *gourde* can mean a stupid person as well as a canteen.

that it relies on values that are part of a long tradition in our civilization, going back to the Bible. We find an early reframing of this sort in Isaiah 53:4, where the prophet says, "Surely he hath borne our griefs, and carried our sorrows: yet we did esteem him a leper, smitten of God, and afflicted." And the learned doctors of the Talmud were advancing the same sort of reframing in the Tractate Sanhedrin (Babylonian Talmud, 1935; p. 98b in the Hebrew original) when, citing this passage of Isaiah, they characterize the Messiah as "the leper scholar."

Much more recently, Frank Capra's 1946 film *It's a Wonderful Life* gives us another example of the same sort of reframing. As he is going to a river to kill himself, the hero of the film, played by James Stewart, sees a drowning man. Forgetting what he has planned to do, he jumps in and rescues him, only to find that the one he has rescued is none other than his guardian angel, who has used this unusual method to force him out of his suicidal ideas.

It is important for the therapist to treat reframing as a working tool rather than as "the truth." The leap that this kind of intervention allows is useful only if it offers another understanding of the situation, opens other possibilities. If therapists take the position of being firmly anchored in the world of reality and knowing what is "really" happening, they run the risk of taking over from their patients and limiting all their attempts to follow their own truths. These therapists' reframings may also become one-way streets that prevent their patients from finding possibilities in paths that are not therapist's paths. In couple therapy, when I positively reframe the behavior of one partner and accompany the reframing with a paradoxical comment that shows how the behavior protects the other partner's construction of the world, I am only trying to offer a different experience. I simply hope that this experience will allow all the members of the therapeutic system to change. If that happens, the reframing will have turned out to be a useful working tool, but that doesn't mean that it was "true."

Rituals in Couple Therapy

One of the tools I often use in couple therapy is paradoxical tasks that deal with both levels of the partners' double binds *at the same time.* As an example, consider the couple I mentioned in the last chapter. They were seen under my supervision at a university hospital in Brussels.

The wife wanted her husband to "show some feelings" and pay more attention to her. In her family of origin, her mother had paid very little attention to her and had criticized the money she spent, "even when it was reasonable," and her father dared pay any attention to her only behind her mother's back. She felt that he had let her down when she was eighteen: she wasn't allowed to come home from her boarding school on weekends because she was "in the way" and "the train was too expensive."

The husband wanted his wife to show a little tenderness and appreciate him more. In his family of origin he had felt like an unwanted child and had experienced himself as "an orphan." He told the therapist, "My mother rejected me; my grandmother let me down," and added, "I endured a total lack of affection, of tenderness, of attention."

Following my model, the wife on the level of her official program wanted her husband to "show some feelings" and pay attention to her, but at the same time on the level of her world view she thought she could only be in the way and believed that no one could pay attention to her. And the husband on one level wanted her to be tender and appreciate him more, but never having had that experience in childhood he was unable to believe that he could ever get what he wanted. Neither spouse could try to satisfy the other's stated wishes without running into the other side of the double bind. Here are some extracts from a session where the therapist suggested some paradoxical tasks.

THERAPIST [*To the wife*]: What do you want from your husband?

WIFE: For him to show some feelings. To spend an hour a week with me. To stop sitting there like a bump on a log.

THERAPIST: And what do you want from your wife?

HUSBAND: For her to appreciate what I do . . . to show a little tenderness.

THERAPIST: Can you spell that out more?

HUSBAND: I want her to stop arguing with me every time I say something. I want her to stop complaining. Her complaining drives me up the wall. She's systematically destroying me; I want her to stop that and start being constructive. [*At this point the therapist took a break and went behind the one-way mirror. After a discussion, she returned.*]

THERAPIST: I'm going to ask you to do something that may not work. My colleagues in the back room don't think it will work.

[*To the husband*]: Your wife wants you to spend an hour a week with her. I'm going to ask you to set aside half an hour, twice a week, when you'll be free and can pay attention to her. I want you to take this time to be with her, in spite of what I'm going to ask her to do.

[*To the wife*]: For your part, I want you to tell him you don't want it, that just because I asked him to do it doesn't mean you have to accept it.

HUSBAND: There's an obvious contradiction there.

THERAPIST [*To the wife*]: You should refuse because he doesn't do it when you ask him. He'll only be doing it because I've asked him to. . . . And as for you, I want you to show him some tenderness.

WIFE: But he pushes me away.

THERAPIST [*To the husband*]: When she's tender with you, I want you to be very careful not to be touched by it.

WIFE: He's like that already!

The therapist repeated the homework and asked them both to note what they experienced.

She learned in the next session that the wife had cooked for her husband and had written him a loving note. He had thanked her, saying it was too bad it didn't happen more often, but then he realized that this was exactly the homework his wife had been asked to do. In spite of this, the wife continued to give attention to her husband.

The husband told the therapist, "It was a little ray of light." The wife agreed and added, "We talked till three in the morning two nights running. . . . He was gentle and kind of blissful, he'd grown ten years younger. He was the way I used to know him ten years ago."

Up until that point, if her husband paid attention to her, she didn't believe him and pushed him away. He would then withdraw and she would complain about his withdrawal. And if the wife displayed tenderness toward him and showed him that she cared for him, the husband didn't believe her either because her behavior would call into question his world view. This of course meant that his wife felt rejected and he could continue to complain about not being appreciated. Thanks to these tasks that prescribed to each of them what they were already doing, the therapist freed each of them from the double binds they were caught in.

In the context of this prescription, each member of the couple could experience both levels of the double bind internally without having to see the spouse as the aggressor. If someone was setting a trap, it was no longer the partner but the therapist. If there had to be a jailer, it was no longer the other member of the couple but the therapist with her crazy homework.

It is obvious that what happened in the therapy was much more complex than I have described. If the therapist constructed her model of their reciprocal double binds around these particular issues, it is perhaps because these were close to issues in her own life, too. As a result change was produced on the level of the whole therapeutic system and not just on the level of the couple.

On the other hand, tasks like this are only an episode in the therapeutic process, which can also fail. For scarcely will an increased flexibility appear in one area than a new difficulty will show up somewhere else. Whatever people who would like to see the psychotherapist as some kind of magician may think, in most cases the therapeutic system has to settle in to a long and difficult piece of work.

Self-reference as the Therapist's Trump Card

Pondering the different examples of self-reference given in this book, the reader may be wondering how it is possible to escape such situations. For me, the solution is not to escape self-reference but to use it as the heart of the therapy. For this reason I suggest that therapists should respect the following points.

1. Accept the fact that feelings arising in us are not uniquely the result of our own history. They also have a meaning and a function with respect to the therapeutic system.

2. Be skeptical about them. If we follow the feelings that arise in us without checking out the echo in the members of the couple or family, we can run into two kinds of difficulty: (a) It is always possible in a given situation that our experience is indeed more connected to our own history than it is to the experience of the other members of the therapeutic system. (b) If we follow our feeling without caution, we run the strong risk of confirming our own world view and the world views of the family members. If this happens we will set up a system

where the more things change the more they remain the same.

3. Check whether what we are feeling has a function both in relation to both the members of the couple or of the family and to ourselves. If this turns out to be the case, we will have discovered a unique and special bridge between the members of the couple or family and ourselves. We will be changing ourselves at the same time that we are helping the other members of the therapeutic system to change. In trying to modify world views similar to our own, we will be participating in a shared enterprise of liberation. The task will prove easier to the extent that the elements from our own past are different from those of the family members, since this will counterbalance the possible similarities of the deep beliefs that we share.

4. The work of therapy consists in freeing up the elements that appear at the intersection of the different universes of the members of the therapeutic system. The way this is done and the conditions under which the therapist will be able to change at the same time as the members of the couple or family will depend on the therapist's underlying theoretical school. What is important for me is not so much the underlying theory as the fit between the theory and the members of the therapeutic system.

I have suggested as best I can my own constructions concerning the possible development of an approach to systemic therapy. If, as a result of I don't know what fortunate intersections, these constructions have been able to connect with yours and helped you catch a glimpse of new perspectives, my effort will not have been in vain.

Epilogue:
A Story of Jh'ha

ONE Friday Jh'ha, the hero of many Moroccan stories, was in the mosque. The faithful begged him to address a few words to them. After trying without success to escape their attentions, he finally turned to them and asked, "Do you know what I am going to say to you?" When they said they didn't, he said, "Well, how can I discuss something you don't know?"

The next Friday the worshipers were ready for him. After he again asked, "Do you know what I am going to say to you?" they chorused, "Yes, we do!' "But then what good would it do to talk to you about it?" he replied, and went to sit quietly down among the congregation.

The third Friday they finally thought they had the way to make him talk. When he asked his usual, "Do you know what I am going to say to you?" half the people cried "No!" and the other half cried "Yes!" "Well then," said Jh'ha, "let the ones who do know tell the ones who don't!"

Appendix A
Openness: A Round-Table Discussion

THIS is the transcript of a round table that I organized in 1980 to address areas of mutual interest to family therapists and the Prigogine group.* In addition to Ilya Prigogine and myself, participants were the French psychoanalyst Félix Guattari and two members of the Prigogine group, Isabelle Stengers and Jean-Louis Deneubourg. A glossary at the end of the transcript defines some of the terms used by the participants.

Equifinality and Fluctuations

Mony Elkaïm

I should like first of all to thank you for having been kind enough to set aside time for this round-table discussion. We hope to publish the transcript in the third issue of our *Cahiers* devoted to research in the area of family therapies.

I should like to introduce the discussion by saying a few words about the link between family therapies and the so-called systemic approaches and to explain the importance, as

*The transcript originally appeared in *Cahiers Critiques de Thérapie Familiale et de Pratiques de Réseaux* (No. 3, 1980), and in this English translation in *Family Process* 21 (No. 1, 1982): 57–70.

we see it, of the work of your group for our field of inquiry.

It was in the 1950s that family therapies appeared on the scene in the United States. Therapists had of their own accord begun to see whole families in order to deal with the problem of one of their members.

These therapists then began to discover extremely interesting things. They found out, for example, that when the identified patient began to get better, another member of the family might get worse. They were gradually prompted by a whole series of elements of that sort to ask themselves to what extent certain laws that were generally valid for open systems might not be extrapolated to family systems.

There followed a number of research projects centered at Palo Alto and conducted by Bateson, Jackson, Haley, Weakland, Watzlawick, and their associates. One of the things they attempted to do was to see whether they could apply concretely the work done on open systems in general and that of Bertalanffy in particular to therapeutic work with families.

The members of that group thus took up a series of concepts such as totality, equifinality and homeostasis, in particular, and attempted to determine how they might apply them when tackling a problem and inquiring into the function of that problem in a system, and in so doing might devise a different clinical approach from that traditionally used for psychiatric problems. Theoretically there was room for positive feedback and amplification. In fact, however, this was largely lip service, rather than an actual development in theoretical elaboration.

Although Bertalanffy himself insisted that cybernetics and homeostasis were merely individual chapters in the theory of open systems and tried to avoid having his approach reduced to these elements, that is in fact what happened in our field.

Our work, which is geared to change, took place in a theoretical context that was based essentially on an assumption of stability.

It is in this respect that we find your research so significant.

In so far as it has helped us to think in terms of systems opened by flows that keep them open, of dissipative structures that may come into being through bifurcations at points away from the thermodynamic equilibrium, your work has opened up interesting avenues for us to explore. This holds good even if research in this field is clearly, for our purposes, only at a comparatively embryonic stage.

The elements we have taken from your work and that we have started to use are, in particular:

- the idea of a distance from equilibrium, which at a given moment, through amplification, permits a bifurcation;
- the aspect of randomness in the choice of fluctuation that invades the field;
- the evolutionary feedback aspect that makes it possible to go from one state to another.

For the benefit of our readers, I should like this discussion to serve as an introduction to your work and as a means of discussing the usefulness or danger you think could ensue from attempting to use your research to account for processes of self-organisation and change in the area of family systems and even perhaps, in a broader manner, in the area of certain human systems.

Ilya Prigogine

The development you have presented seems to me to be fairly parallel to that of ideas in the physical and chemical spheres. Moreover, there have been some interactions between the two ways of thinking, particularly with Bertalanffy, since 1945 or 1946. It was way back in 1928 that De Donder's disciples introduced the concept of "open system" that has since been taken up by Bertalanffy. He took a keen interest in the theorem of minimum entropy production that I established in 1945 and that he advanced as an example of equifinality. If I specify this, it is not in order to detract from Bertalanffy's importance but merely to point out that the interaction already existed at the time. For my part, I soon realized that the minimum entropy production theorem was not sufficient to deal with the problem of living objects, because it led to contemplating evolution toward a state that would be insensitive to fluctuation. Whether it be a matter of the state of equilibrium corresponding to maximum entropy or that corresponding to minimum entropy production in conditions close to equilibrium, nothing new can happen; that is in fact the very meaning of the concept of equifinality. Whatever conditions may be at the outset, the system evolves toward the same state, which is a state immune to its own fluctuations. There is thus no escape.

Now, what I found to be obvious for natural systems, that singular events may entail new processes, seems to me to be equally true in your field. We are going through something new; perhaps it is even the very first impression of our psychological existence—for example, when we have the impression of having solved a problem. It is a very strong impression, and it need not necessarily concern a highly intellectual problem. We come to a new viewpoint. We have the feeling: "Of course! From this moment, from 6 o'clock in the morning, I've understood that in this or that circumstance, I should think in a different way." In a way, the classical conception denied this experience, reduced it to an artifact, an illusion, as in anything new. The impression of novelty, it was argued, was bound up with the fact that we do not possess all the data, that we have only a limited knowledge of what goes on in our brain. What astounds me is that people who have a profound knowledge of neurophysiology say the same thing—for example, Jean-Pierre Changeux in his inaugural address at the Collège de France, when he said that there is no doubt that determinism is universal and applies equally to the brain as to an atomic system.

Here lies the whole issue of what is reality and what is illusion. Should we abandon that "illusion" in favor of the "realities" sanctioned by that science, or should we rethink that reality and perhaps come to a concept of reality separated by a less deep chasm from that very strongly felt impression that runs through our existence? I believe that it is in the latter direction that we are moving, and we think that the patterns of reality put to us by classical physics were oversimplified. Thus, the concept of law was too strongly opposed to that of chance. We are now coming to a somewhat more qualified and therefore somewhat less artificial view of things.

What Units? What Interactions?

Ilya Prigogine

To remain in the area of generalities for a few minutes and to come to your problem, to speak to you about the family, which is a community, we need, from our point of view, to know the link between the possible component units of that community and the collective behavior. As long as we thought in terms of very simple interactions such as gravitation, there was really no problem in defining the units. For example, gravitation does not prevent us from speaking of the earth and the sun as objects clearly having their own characteristics independent of their interaction. Now, certain situations can lose the simplicity that already obtains at the stage of physics or chemistry. Let us take what I believe has been one of the most important experiments of the last fifteen years or so, the chemical clock. What are involved are chemical reactions whose presence is evidenced in different colorations of the medium. We see the latter change color from time to time. But we can also obtain with strictly similar units, that is molecules, albeit under slightly different conditions, a whole range of other structures, from spatial structures to chemical waves. Thus, confronted with different collective behaviors, we may always ask ourselves whether the units at work are not the same. I believe that is a fundamental problem. Take an example that comes to my mind. Compare an African society with a European society. The differences are obvious, but should we reduce them to differences between units or between interactions as they have evolved and stabilized themselves in institutions, which in their turn react on the individual, in particular, by creating transmissible states of things? For my part, rather than speak about differences between men, I would prefer to speak of differing stabilizations of interactions between them, that is to say—metaphorically, of course—of societies corresponding to different branches of solutions to a system of nonlinear equations. In the past, I believe we overestimated the weight of units and underestimated that of interactions. It is in this context, I believe, that your problem should be located. However, a mere catalogue of what there is in common with other problems will clearly not suffice.

As far as we are concerned, we need to see how far we can go in formulating nonlinear interactions. But, at all events, I believe that the introduction of a terminology may have some effect on the orientation of a work. For example, Freudian psychoanalysis is not a "hard science," but it was of great importance in the development of our ways of thinking. Stating certain problems in terms of interaction, of stabilizations that also act finally on the individual, of different collective forms of behavior may help to prompt new explorations.

Félix Guattari

In the field of human sciences, there are two ways of using references to the exact sciences and to the sciences of nature: either by directly making operational borrowings from them or by using them as a sort of conceptual superego. One would need to embark on the history of oppressive scientific references to show to what extent they are able to bar the way to, or even forbid, certain advances, not only in practice but—more seriously—in our minds. That the dismantling of this scientific superego should involve science itself, physicians, and particularly you and your team is, I believe, very good news. To some extent, it is, I think, the explanation for the attention, the success and even perhaps the uproar that was unleashed by the papers you published recently. Indeed, if my assumption is correct, namely that a superego of this type does exist somewhere, it may be supposed that it will operate in the most varied fields and that all sorts of bodies will come to its aid as soon as it feels threatened.

Your latest book is an instrument of the first order in helping us to rid ourselves of classic concepts concerning causality and time. I think we should refrain, however, from believing that we shall be able to derive miraculous solutions from what you put forward, for example, for analysis of family systems, psychoanalytic complexes, and the like. The idea precisely is not to use your scientific achievements in order to carry out massive transfers of enunciations that would function as so many dogmas.

I should like to revert to two problems you have just referred to in your introductory statement, in order to illustrate what I think to be the "proper usage" of what you have to contribute. The first relates to the concept of *unit* and the second to that of *interaction*. Particle physics, if I understand you correctly, has had to break away from a physics of trajectories of well-defined objects to accede to a physics of interactions between processes whose unitary character is far less plainly visible.

Interactions is a word on everybody's lips these days. But interactions of what with what? Interactions between what types of groups? For example, the existence of individual interactions within a family seems to be self-evident. But we do not ask ourselves whether we are really dealing with individuals in a family or in any social grouping.

Is a child just as much an individual as a wife, a pater familias, and so on? It is, of course, possible to detect biological individualism. To what extent, however, may we speak of interactions between individuals?

Are we so sure that when a speaker speaks, he speaks only from himself? Do spoken words or symptoms not essentially involve elements that fall short of the individual (organic, physiological, sensory, dreaming, and other functions) and elements that are contextual (father's profession, socioeconomic factors, etc.)?

An individual's behavior is said to be aggressive or inhibited. But what is aggressive? What does inhibited mean? To what mythical unitary entity do we relate such segments of behavior?

The concept of individual unity strikes me as misleading. To claim on the basis of such a unity to be able to center a system of interactions between behaviors arising in fact out of heterogeneous components that cannot unequivocally be located in one person appears to me to be an illusion. It is in this respect that I find your questions most useful. More particularly, your concept of "internal times" could come to play an essential role in challenging the globalistic, reifying concept of the individual. The idea would be to found on the "internal times" concept not only an "internal age" depending upon a single biological clock, but also rhythms, rhymes, and a whole range of tempi that coexist within an entity that is called an individual subject.

If I may say so, the interactions we are dealing with in this field are *semiotic interactions,* with or without subjective effects, accompanied or not by conscious effects generating a feeling of individualism.

Semiotic productions may lead to mere redundancies of significance, but they may also be the subject of "dissipative" processes: semiotic interactions "away from equilibrium," entailing an upheaval of dominant systems of redundancy. We should therefore reconsider all former interactions (between the signs themselves, between the signs and the material and emotional processes), inasmuch as they initiate transformations, generate new realities and affects.

It is by taking on board this type of interaction—which I refer to incidentally as "diagrammatics"—that we should be better able to apprehend the problem area or systems and what I have called machinic arrangements and enunciative dispositions. It is with this type of interaction as our starting point, remote from redundant equilibria, that we shall be able to reappraise the *particular cases* of closed, stratified, and relatively open structures, for example, in the field of intrafamily communications. As I see it, only borderline cases are involved, in the sense that you say that the physics of trajectories is a borderline case of the physics of interactions. Systemic interactions, highly formalized by certain family therapists, are also only borderline cases in which, under certain conditions, a number of semiotic interactions and subjectivations are located off field. They are nonetheless interesting for that!

Ilya Prigogine

I quite agree with these remarks. A great deal of work is required to articulate the points of view from which we set out and which are very different. Our point of view is partly conditioned by the fact that, historically speaking, physics conceived of units as having priority compared with interactions. That goes back a long way. In my book written with Isabelle Stengers, we speak about systems integratable in dynamics; these are the simple systems that so far have to a large extent served as a model for the description of the ideal physics. Now these systems can be described in terms of units without interactions; or, by way of reference to Leibniz, they can be called monadic, with all interactions eliminated. Each unit evolves separately as if it were alone in the world. For fifty years the quantum theory has been attempting to take up this monadic viewpoint, that is, to eliminate interactions in order to define particles without reference to them as ideal beings to which the interaction is subsequently added. Our point of view is not original in itself; a philosopher such as Whitehead, to quote only him, laid much stress on the fact that individuals define themselves in a field of action, that they are not separable from the entirety of their interactions, except in extremely simplified cases that might be termed degenerate in the physical sense (a degenerate system is a qualitatively impoverished system compared with other systems of its kind; a series of distinctions about it is useless, a series of information redundant). In this sense, the systems of classical physics correspond to borderline cases, and the modes of description appropriate to them generally do not permit extrapolation.

Thus, in emphasizing the interactions, our purpose is to relativize those of the individual. In a sense, the individual is by way of becoming himself. He does not enter into a process without himself being changed in nature. Even the elementary particles have been formed; they are not the eternal foundation of the universe but the carriers of a thermodynamic evolution that is in process.

In regard to social interactions, that is a problem I had occasion to address some years ago when I concerned myself with motor traffic. How should one put the problem to oneself? People drive in town or on a motorway. What can theory do about it? A theory worthy of the name should make it possible to predict a behavior, but how can one predict a behavior in such a complex system that can be approached from so many different angles? In the particular instance, I did not attempt to derive a system "in the absolute" that would provide me with an interpretation of the traffic as such; I tried to determine how this complex behavior might respond to slightly modified conditions. The same applies to all complex situations. Take your therapy problems. What would an "absolute" theory boil down to? Chemistry? Food? The structure of society? For me, the theoretical question was: What will happen in this group if certain conditions of life are changed? And a reply to such a question is quite interesting.

In the case of motor traffic, I am not going to ask myself why Mr. X wants to go at 75 mph, whereas Mr. Y, admiring the landscapes, drives at 40 mph. If I enter into those interactions, I am lost. I thus have to take an overall viewpoint and tell myself: I know the distribution of the speeds at which people want to drive, the speed they would drive at if they were alone on the road, and I ask myself how their interactions will modify their ability to achieve their goals. In the case of societies, I think it can be said that, without nonlinear interactions in the mathematical sense, it is practically impossible to define a society, regardless of whether the interactions are imitation or anti-imitation, such as those that were studied by Deneubourg or the semiotic interactions you were mentioning. Society seems to me to be an irreducible concept; one cannot reduce it to well-defined units in the manner of Leibniz's monads. And, of course, the problem of a social group cannot be isolated from its context. The problem of a Jewish family in the Soviet Union is probably posed in a different manner from that of an Arab family on the West Bank. That does not mean that no social phenomenon can be studied; we must try to isolate the variables, identify the relevant interactions, but we should be wary of universal theories.

Isabelle Stengers

To bring out the way the two viewpoints interrelate, one can say that, when we make a theory concerning the way a system will react to this or that modification, we make a choice. In fact, we make a decision concerning the systemic nature of the fragment of reality we are dealing with. In so doing, of course, we take a risk: it may happen that the definition we decide to give to the system will merely endorse a situation determined by various social, cultural, and political pressures and that, instead of understanding it, we blindly freeze into a coherent system something that had other virtualities. Let us take a "family" problem, that is to say something that presents itself in an obvious way as being of the family order. I may ask myself how the situation will evolve if I change this or that parameter that defines the system as a family system, or I may ask myself whether other virtualities are present. I can attempt, despite the "obviousness," to recall that the units are involved not only in family interactions but in all sorts of other interactions, the number of which is perhaps indefinite. This choice is perhaps not familiar to the practitioner who is accustomed to considering the problem as given. It implies responsibilities, therapeutic or political. We have to know whether we are confirming the problem as it is given or whether we are trying to open it up a little more, to give it a few additional degrees of freedom. What is often frozen is not only such and such a situation, but the definition of the problem that presents itself to the therapist.

Stability and Multistationarity

Mony Elkaïm

As I see it, we are really at the crux of what we are concerned with. The impression I have long had with the systemic models we use is that they are models that account for what happens in a somewhat unsophisticated (but not necessarily wrong) manner that could be summarized as follows: The family system is caught between two forces; a force that leads in the direction of change—because, say, the youngest adolescent child has to leave home, or, after emigration to a country with a very different culture, one has to change certain patterns of living—and a force that tends to preserve the internal equilibrium.

An attempt would then be made to understand the symptom as having a function to protect the homeostasis, by allowing the old rigid rules that might be anachronistic to continue to operate in order to avoid for the family the danger that change might represent.

We were however ill equipped to take into account the singularities that we were able to link up to our system. Something highly interesting then happened: We read in the system only what connected with what we put into it, and that very soon led to a reductionist view of things.

Our colleagues who argued with us then warned us: "If you increase the number of parameters, you may become paralyzed. If you draw a map as complex as the territory it depicts, there will be no map and you will get lost in the middle of the territory."

The problem then arose for us in the terms in which you expressed it: The fact that the problems we encounter cannot be isolated from their context does not mean that they cannot be studied, but how can we, while not trusting in general theories, isolate the variables?

Could we not study what Félix Guattari calls the "origin in praxis" of a situation? Could we not, if we do not look for certain singularities with a wealth of virtual systems, at least give these singularities a chance? How can we bring a system to a point fairly remote from its equilibrium in order to create a context in which the elements that may enable the system to change its state can be amplified?

Jean-Louis Deneubourg

The process you describe is an example of multiple states. Multistationarity is a type of organization that is fairly easy to achieve from the theoretical standpoint and is very widespread in biochemistry, zoology, etc. It is the simultaneous existence, for a given value of each of the system's parameters, of several possible solutions. Take a simple situation: the existence of three stationary solutions, including one stable and two unstable ones. If we take a mechanical image, that of a marble rolling in a landscape featured by two valleys and a peak, the marble can move in that geography, the three stationary states being the valley bottoms (stable states) and the mountain top (the unstable state).

If I nudge it gently, the marble that is in the bottom of one of the valleys will move a short distance up the side of the valley before rolling back into it. This situation is the image of your homeostatic system, a situation for which fluctuations, random events, are cushioned and "erased." On the contrary, if my marble is at the top of the hill, the slightest shock will be amplified by the geography of the system, and the marble will end up in the valley below.

If I now return to the situation in which my marble is in the bottom of one of the valleys, the valley not being very deep, a slight shock will cause the marble to fall back into that valley, whereas if the shock is sufficiently violent, the marble will be projected over the crest and into the other valley. With the latter phenomenon, we have the image of a critical disturbance.

The passage from one valley to the other can take place in another manner: simply by following "the bed of the rivers that flow through the two valleys." If I am in one of the valleys, I can go downstream to where the two rivers join and then work my way up the second valley. This "technique" corresponds to the change of state through the variation of one of the parameters of the system. For example, I increase the value of the parameter, then having reached the point where the rivers meet, I diminish it to the initial value, but I am now in the second valley and I remain there.

In order to illustrate change of structure through a variation of parameters, I will take the example of the construction of galleries by termites, a phenomenon that is also no doubt multistationary. For an inflow of insects, a gallery of a given width is built. If now, for whatever reason, the insect flow in the gallery happens to increase, several new solutions can be proposed. A new gallery of larger dimensions can be built, or a lateral gallery can be added to the first. The choice is determined by the conditions and the nature of the environment, but also no doubt by chance: it is sufficient that some insects should have initiated a lateral gallery in a quite random way for the process to be amplified; on the contrary, if it is the substitution phenomenon that is initiated, the first gallery will be replaced by a single, bigger gallery.

The Choice of Models

Isabelle Stengers

Here we have to note a somewhat ironic contrast. The scientist dealing with ants is looking for a certain kind of success, which is perfectly proper; he will be happy if he manages to reduce the complicated problem of a termite hill to a small set of interactions described by a small number of equations giving a certain variety of collective behaviors. In that sense, which is ideal for the scientist, it is the extreme situation. But it should be taken in the sense that, say, the trajectories constitute a limit that does not lend itself automatically to extrapolation to all dynamic situations in which we have a given set of equations in which all interactions between termites are at work all the time but produce different global consequences from case to case. That, by the way, is not necessarily the case with termites, but it *is* the case with the multistationary states to which Jean-Louis was referring. Now this ideal, I believe, constitutes an illegitimate temptation for specialists, in human societies. And this is true, even if "it works"—that is, if you act effectively on individuals by supposing them to be endowed with only "gross" family, social, or other relations and by trying on that basis to reshape their world.

Ilya Prigogine

The dangerous temptation would be to reduce the individual to too small a thing: here, even with a thing that is small, one can succeed in constructing highly interesting, complex structures. The greater the number of possible varieties of behavior, the greater the social wealth. To my mind, one of the essential points has always been pluralism. In this variegated society, we must succeed in achieving multiple vocations, and I attach great importance to the link between what each one of us does and what is being built globally.

Félix Guattari

Basically, we are confronted with a problem of choice of models concerning the unconscious. I was much struck by

Isabelle Stengers' remark about the temptation to reconstitute complex social situations starting from a basis of "gross relations." What is at stake here is a model of unconscious representation that would be finalized as objectives whose representation no particular person possesses. That sort of system should appeal to a certain ideal of capitalism, and not only liberal capitalism either!

Despite their statistical disorder, all individual behaviors contribute in some degree to a certain finality. Centralization agencies exist, but they have to respect the zones of statistical choice. What dominates, what wins the day when this pseudo-democracy has played itself out? That is another question.

We cannot deny the existence of such models around us. For instance, the model of the mass media, TV, is something that strongly resembles your termite tales. We come here to a certain "softly, softly, catchee monkey" modelization, without any visible orchestration that spells out the targets to be attained. You get the impression that it works all on its own. We can thus refer to a certain type of model of the unconscious or, if you prefer, a model of semiotization on a collective scale.

Then, on the other hand, we come back to the little differences that propel the marble, that cause the mutation of the molecular link and the proliferation of the system. Here we are confronted with another type of choice and another model of the unconscious.

It is no longer numbers that directly lay down the law; it is micro-mutation that generates numbers and recasts the law. In your book you refer to this in terms almost of "local disorder."

What is this singularity, this marble that takes power, that decides not for all but on account of an all that is in process of being constituted? In what measure is it the carrier of potential model transformations? Can we forge the instruments of a science of singular interactions? That brings us to the very heart of the problem of family (or any other) therapy. That is what is at stake. Either we continue to import enunciations external to the dispositions concerned, which for their part unceasingly produce specific systems in order to adapt or to refuse the dominant systems by reason of their "fixations" at certain points of singularity, or we agree without any mental reservations to work with these local systems, these systems of singularity.

In the former case, the theory leads to a strengthening of the power groups that are interested in a policy of standardization and who feel the need for such support today because of the challenges and even the breakdown of many psychological and psychoanalytical theories. We will be giving our approval to practices for the manipulation of individuals, families, social groups.

In the latter case, we will make use of research in various fields (ethology and ecology and like fields) in order better to shed light on what the dispositions are in terms, first, of a structure subservient to the dominating systems and, second, as a machine for enunciation and production capable of managing its own fate.

Ilya Prigogine

I should like to lay stress on certain general conclusions to which we are led by the study of our systems, however simple the latter may be.

The first conclusion is that we must make a clear-cut distinction between stabilization of an amplified fluctuation and optimalization. Not every amplification leads to an optimalization and, up to a point, if one can speak sometimes in the light of history, amplification seems to occur in those cases in which a society becomes caught up in situations that, viewed from the outside, at any rate, are horrible. That is the case, for example, of the Aztec civilization, which produced such oustanding art and became embroiled in customs that were so cruel that we find them almost impossible to understand nowadays. Thus, amplification and optimalization do not necessarily overlap. The second conclusion is that insistence on nonlinearity leads to a better appreciation of the wealth of reality, a wealth that is in contradiction with the ideal of a single point of view that is privileged over reality. There is no such thing as the Leibnizian "best possible of all worlds," definable by a single criterion. Leibniz has often been caricatured, but in the most modern physics we also find a search for an optimum. The dynamic study of a physical system was done on the basis of a variational principle such, for example, as that expressed by Lagrange.[1]

But this best of worlds that was the outcome of Lagrangian dynamics finally turns out to be an illusion, a schematization that does not make sufficient allowance for the complexity of the interactions. I believe there is no longer any conceptual possibility of constructing such a criterion. There is a series of possible worlds, and we can become aware of them, albeit through very limited models. That is what is most important, at least from the epistemological point of view. Even in the theory of elementary particles, we speak now of broken symmetry, and we come to conceive the universe as corresponding to one of the possible branches. It is thought that at a given point there was a symmetry that was broken by the initial cooling down of the earth.

But the example I prefer is that of climate. Until about ten or fifteen years ago there existed a classic conception of climate that held that climate was imposed upon us. There was only one possible world, ours. The greater heat or cold experienced at certain periods was determined inevitably by the intensity of the solar fluxes. We believe today that for a given solar flux there are many possible solutions, many climates,

[1] French physicist and mathematician of the second half of the 18th century.

some hot, others not. We suddenly discover that perhaps one day we shall be able to live in a snow-covered world or in a world with a better rainfall distribution. That means that the role of knowledge is becoming more important. We are only at the beginning, at the prehistory of our insights. A contrast often used to be made between the pluralism of social systems and the static character of nature. It was thought societies were different because of man, whereas the environment was given and we had to live and die in it. That idea has now come under attack. The world is richer than we used to think and much more complex. I do not think this is an imperialistic conclusion, but rather the preparation for a different view of things.

Jean-Louis Deneubourg

The model of the termites was quoted only in order to illustrate multi-stationarity and without any desire to transfer or to apply it to other areas. We can continue to discuss the relations between insects and politics at the pub on the corner, although I will quote an anecdote from Gould.[2] At the Free Enterprise stand at the New York World's Fair in 1964, he had seen an ant hill with the caption: "Twenty million years of stagnation in evolution. Why? Because the ant hill is a socialist and totalitarian system."

Two can start a collective; the dynamic theory of games is an example of something that is fairly close to the ideas that have been developed here. Take, for example, systems that have two or three players who make very complex decisions. The way they make their decisions involves a large number of factors, and in such a system we may also observe a collective structure appear, the existence of cycles, etc. That is

[2]Stephen J. Gould, biologist, author of *Ever Since Darwin*, New York, W. W. Norton, 1977.

to say, we need not necessarily resort to the concept of large numbers of individual decisions. You can have hosts of simple, individual decisions and the appearance of an order on a mass scale. On the other hand, these simple decisions may be local and succeed one another, accumulate in the course of time, and the global order may appear when there are only a few people involved.

Managing in Common

Félix Guattari

We may need to manage in common certain concepts, certain notions, even certain studies.

Also, and perhaps first and foremost, a micro-policy for science, particularly in the area of the scientific superego I was mentioning earlier. Science holds sway in every field, even in everyday life, in thinking, in individual desires. We have to acknowledge that in this area the scientific community has become the equivalent of a sort of universal church. Not a single utterance by a head of state or by anyone in a position of responsibility fails to be put to a scientific *authority*.

Even if only by way of implication, any scientific ideology vectors a certain conception of determinism and thus of freedom.

A change of approach such as the one you advocate and that would lead in particular to adopting another policy in relation to singularities, internal times, zones of choice, the creativity of processes away from equilibrium (which cuts across, I think, what I called a micro-policy of molecular interactions) could have incalculable consequences (in more ways than one!).

Ilya Prigogine

You are quite right. I think the concepts we are talking about offer a sort of intellectual framework capable of housing many problems. I quoted the example of climate. Our research has henceforth another orientation because it is oriented toward ideas of instability, multiple states, etc. It is true, however, that in each case, many investigations are necessary in order to enable us to know how to build appropriate models. Your remark coincides with the reason why we spoke in our book about metamorphosis of science. We believe that there are many signs that nature is no longer considered merely manipulatable, that scientific theory is ceasing to be the theory of a passive object. Our relations with nature are no longer the same and, correlatively, we no longer describe science as a rupture. The change is considerable, and you were not wrong to mention the resistance it arouses. Take Antoine Danchin[3] or René Thom,[4] whose contribution to mathematics I gladly acknowledge. For him what we propose is an anti-science. According to him, science should seek to go beyond situations in which hazard and necessity are inseparable, in which rational treatment leads us to acknowledge an irreducible component of the unpredictable, those situations in which we for our part acknowledge that science and manipulation are no longer identical.

I believe also that a new unity is growing up between the various ways of considering nature, in particular between science and ecology. Hostility is strong. Many of the things we say in physics, too, could have been said long ago but they would have been treated with great contempt. It is not so easy to be contemptuous today, however, because we possess data, we have the chemical clock, we have the residual radiation of

---

[3]French contemporary mathematician, author of the "Catastrophe Theory."
[4]French contemporary molecular biologist.

the black body that bears witness to the history of the universe, we have our information on termites. It cannot then be said that all this is "a figment of the imagination;" we have to seek new causal laws, go beyond appearances toward a new unitary theory. We should not think we are in a majority, however, for we are clearly a minority in the present prospect of science. Whether that is for better or worse, I cannot say.

Jean-Louis Deneubourg

Chemists or physicists have no imperialist urge to transfer the mechanisms they have observed in their own disciplines to other areas of society or biology. It is a matter of respecting the specific mechanisms of each of the phenomena studied. Thus, in discussions with an experimenter, one of the first questions the model builder asks is: "What do you see, what mechanisms have you observed?"

The quality of the model outlined, as well as the results derived from it, are of course closely bound up with the quality of the analysis the experimenter is able to provide.

Isabelle Stengers

I want to highlight the pitfall of what I will call the theoretical jubilation. It is great fun, it is very pleasant to reduce a complex phenomenon to a much less limited grouping such as interactions between termites. Thus, theoretical jubilation amounts to saying to oneself that a small number of equations may produce such and such a termite, or such and such another under other circumstances. From there, as Professor Prigogine emphasized, you can have increased respect for the manifoldness of reality, but you can also convert the theoretician's legitimate pleasure into a general methodological rule applicable in areas in which interactions are not one-way or are more ambiguous. In that case, pleasure is transformed into something rather like a policy of flattening out ambivalent interactions into interactions signifying only one thing and that, by definition, will contribute a given system.

Ilya Prigogine

I believe such a totalitarian policy offers less of a temptation when you understand the many possibilities of amplification and when you come across an unexpected richness, precisely when you are not dealing with men but with climate, for example.

Mony Elkaïm

I should like to add a few words particularly for the benefit of Félix. I share your criticism of a reductionist systemic approach, but for me the thermodynamics of states of non-equilibrium are of interest precisely because they help one *not* to be closed to the emergence of heterogeneous singularities within a system.

Indeed, to the importance of rules accounting for the self-organization of a system in a given state of that system, what you call the stratified part of a disposition, should be added the possibilities of amplification of hardly perceptible elements that however become decisive for the subsequent state of the system. In this connection, it might be useful to add that for us, also, amplification does not imply optimalization. Moreover, it is frequently as a result of an amplification process that the symptom occupies the position it does in the family system for which therapy is sought.

That is why I have the impression that this timorous approach to a systemic view of things does not give sufficient credit to the importance and the originality of the work that opens up avenues for use precisely so that we may perhaps avoid reducing to a preconceived system a whole series of elements we are not able to encode.

Félix Guattari

If it is a matter of an antisystemic system, then everything is fine and new horizons will open up in order to shed light on a host of problems concerning modes of semiotization, awareness, etc.

Open Systems: What Openness?

Isabelle Stengers

Summarizing briefly what has been said, I think we can distinguish three meanings of the term "openness." The three meanings seem to me to be in current use, but they are occasionally confused, leading to various misunderstandings. Let us take the first meaning. Mony said that Bertalanffy is opposed to cybernetics. Quite true, but only in that cybernetics considers the technical montage and its functioning separately. The mechanisms of homeostasis, more particularly, are included in the construction and are thus preexistent to the functioning. But, protests Bertalanffy, living beings function in a permanent state of flux; there is no fixed part that could be assimilated to the parts of the electronic circuit; there are only different rates of flux, now faster, now slower. Everything is constantly in a process of renewal—the system is "open." Bertalanffy's triumph was precisely in establishing that this openness does not preclude a certain stability of the system. The open system thus has an equifinal and, therefore predictable, reproducible, stable behavior that is clearly characterizable. Open systems that function in a stable manner and have a recognizable identity, as thus highlighted by Bert-alanffy, are precisely those for which—as is the case when the minimum entropy production theory applies—the equi-final state resembles the state of equilibrium. In short, the openness of the system does not prevent its being known according to a model analogous to that which prevails in re-spect to isolated systems.

The second meaning of the term "openness" is linked in a positive manner to the deviation from equilibrium. This brings us to the area of bifurcations, amplifications of fluc-tuation, ruptures of symmetry, and structured functioning systems. This time, not only does the system exist as a physical object despite its openness, but in fact it lives on its openness. The phenomena studied are of a qualitatively new type and exist only on account of the fluxes that traverse the system and move it away from equilibrium. As has just been stressed a number of times, this is where we realize that in slightly different conditions the same equations may produce quali-tatively different results.

But this meaning of "openness" is still very restricted. The system studied is defined by a given set of equations that define once and for all a range of possibilities. That does not appear to be a grave matter in the case of a simple chemical system; there we are convinced we know what chemical events are likely to take place and on what factors their relative frequency depends. All this is written in the shape of a chem-ical equation, and we calculate the consequences. There is no doubt as to the identity of the chemical system as a system; there seems to be no possible choice on the matter.

Now, in many other cases, it is the very definition of the system that gives rise to problems and that supposes a choice. In those cases there is not only openness from the standpoint of interaction with the outside but also openness from the standpoint of the multiplicity of the interactions one can decipher and thus, finally, of the multiplicity of the possible systems these interactions construct. As to the questions what units or what interactions, the choice is not defined in terms of true or false or even of effectiveness in prediction or intervention. For it is not only a matter of recognizing what exists, of detecting the interactions that dominate all the others and that very obviously dominate the functioning. It may also involve giving a chance to other interactions that are practically invisible in the dominant regime and are not included in the definition of the system. About these interactions it may be said that they preexist in a virtual mode or that they occur without specifying where they come from. At all events, they may perhaps assume great importance in another functioning regime. Thus, in the third meaning of "openness," the choice of this or that modelization may be decisive; one assumes the responsibility either of corroborating the importance of a number of interactions as they present themselves or of opening up new possibilities and thus either of confirming all sorts of pressures that have stabilized the domination of those interactions or of helping to create additional degrees of freedom.

For my part, I will assume that this choice in fact exists when one is dealing with a natural object, but it becomes a matter of some urgency in the case of relations between people. Let us revert to the case of the termites. There, also, certain interactions are dominant, and I could decide to help others try their luck to see whether the termites could not build something other than a system-to-build-an-anthill. In doing so, however, I would be running counter to thousands of years of selective pressure that have no doubt stabilized this type of collective behavior. With people, we are dealing with century-old traditions, institutions, lifetimes, decades. The responsibility soon loses a lot of its abstract character.

Definitions

1. *Dissipative Structures.* These structures represent various modes of self-organization in space or time, which, in contrast with equilibrium structures, are maintained only by a flow of energy or matter through the system.
2. *Fluctuations.* Spontaneous deviations away from equilibrium or from a steady state, which occur in any physicochemical system.
3. *Bifurcations.* In mathematics, these phenomena correspond to the abrupt appearance of a new solution for a critical value of a system's parameter.
4. *Evolutionary Feedback.* An increased distance away from equilibrium may lead to the appearance of some dissipative structure; the latter may further increase energy dissipation, favoring thereby the appearance of new structures.
5. *Semiotic Interaction and Diagrammatics.* The diagram is an expression taken from Charles Sanders Peirce (*Principles of Philosophy. Elements of Logic. Collected Papers*, vol. 1. Cambridge, Mass.: Belknap Press of Harvard University Press, 1931). He classifies the diagrams among icons and refers to them as "icons of relations." The diagrammatic interactions (or semiotic interactions), in our own terminology, are opposed to semiotic redundancies. The first make the sign systems work directly with the realities to which they refer, whereas the second simply represent them by giving "equivalents" without an operational effect. For example: mathematical algorithms, technological designs, software referring to the production of a technical object, participate directly in the creative process, whereas an advertisement of the object is only an extrinsic representation.
6. *Machinic Arrangements.* Here the mechanism is distinguished from the machine. The mechanical system is fairly closed within itself; it only has a coded relationship with external "flows." The machines on the contrary, in their historical development constitute phyla comparable to living species.

They create, select, eliminate each other, design new lines of potential. In the broad sense of the term, machines, that is, not only technical machines but also theoretical, social, and aesthetic ones, never function in isolation but in aggregate or in arrangement. A technical machine in a plant, for example, functions in intersection with a social machine, a training machine, a research machine, a trade machine, etc.

7. *Enunciative Disposition*. Linguistic enunciation theories constantly center the linguistic production on individuated subjects, even though language, in essence, is social and, in addition, is diagrammatically connected to the surrounding realities. Beyond the appearance of the individuated enunciation, the real *collective enunciative dispositions* must be discerned. A collective is not to be understood here in the meaning of a social group; it also implies the entry of diverse collections of technical objects, of material and energy flows, subjective noncorporeal objects, mathematical idealities, aesthetics, etc.

8. *Subjectivation*. Here subjectivity is not viewed as something in itself, as something immovable. There is, or there is not, subjectivity of a given nature, depending upon the given enunciative disposition that produces it. For example, modern capitalism, via the media and collective equipment, has produced a new type of subjectivation on a large scale. Some people note, as for the enunciative disposition, that behind the appearance of an individuated subjectivity, it is necessary to seek what the real processes of subjectivation are.

Appendix B
More on Maturana's and Varela's Terms

IN this appendix I present certain major concepts of Maturana and Varela for the benefit of readers who would like a fuller understanding of the ideas I introduce in chapter 3. Some of these concepts I refer to in the body of the book; others, although not mentioned directly, are part of its implicit intellectual context. I am going to talk particularly of "objectivity in quotation marks" or, as Maturana calls it, "objectivity in parentheses" (Maturana, 1983), and their distinction between organization and structure. I shall also define autopoietic systems and structural coupling and describe their use of the terms autonomy, ontogeny, and adaptation.

Maturana (1983) says that scientific explanations are generative explanations, that is, they propose mechanisms that can generate the phenomena under consideration and are acceptable to the scientific community because they satisfy the commonly accepted conditions for valid scientific statements. These conditions, often called collectively the scientific method, are the following.

1. A description of the phenomenon to be explained. This requires a listing of the conditions that an observer must satisfy in his or her experiential domain in order to observe the phenomenon.
2. An explanatory hypothesis, that is, a proposed mechanism

that would generate the phenomenon under consideration.
3. The prediction of at least one other phenomenon that should be generated by the proposed mechanism.
4. The observation of this new phenomenon by an observer satisfying the experiential conditions necessary to make the observation.

Maturana (1983) points out that the scientific method requires internal consistency but not objectivity. A world of objects is not a prerequisite for scientific explanations. All that is necessary is a community of observers whose statements satisfy the conditions listed above. The fact that a scientific explanation can match our perception of the world does not allow us to conclude that there is an objective world independent of the observations of the observer.

It is for this reason that Maturana prefers to speak of "objectivity in quotation marks." For him, our fundamental act as observers is making a distinction. By this operation we separate an entity, or in Maturana and Varela's language a unity, from its environment and affirm that the two are distinct. When we create distinctions, we bring forward a domain of coordinated actions; in this way we generate descriptions and descriptions of descriptions. Necessarily it is the observer who determines what is brought forward in the distinction. And both the observer and the thing being described are present in the language in which the distinction is made. "Matter, metaphorically speaking, is the creation of the spirit (the mode of existence of the observer in a domain of discourse), and . . . spirit is the creation of the matter it creates" (Maturana & Varela, 1980, p. xviii).

In our role as observers we can make a distinction between simple unities and complex unities. The former are unities we do not separate into component parts; the latter are unities where we can make further distinctions. The properties of a complex unity depend on its *organization* and its *structure*.

Concerning organization and structure, Maturana (in press) says: "The organization of a system is defined by the relationship of the components which give it its identity as a class (a chair, a car, a refrigerator factory, a living being, or whatever). The particular way the organization of a given system is arranged—the types of components and the concrete relationships between them—constitutes its structure. The organization of a system is invariant whereas its structure may change."

Maturana points out that the word *organization* comes from the Greek word *organon,* which means instrument. *Organization,* then, refers to the instrumental participation of the components that make up the unity, that is, to the relationship among the components that defines the system *as* a unity. *Structure,* on the other hand, comes from the Latin verb *struere,* which means to construct. It involves the concrete components and the specific relationships these components must assume in order to exist as a unity. For example, "In a toilet the organization of the system of water-level regulation consists in the relations between an apparatus capable of detecting the water level and another apparatus capable of stopping the inflow of water. The toilet unit embodies a mixed system of plastic and metal comprising a float and bypass valve. This specific structure, however, could be modified by replacing the plastic with wood, without changing the fact that there would still be a toilet organization" (Maturana & Varela, 1987, p. 47).

In this sense, according to Maturana (1975), the organization of a complex unity defines it as a unity, determines its properties, and specifies a domain within which it can interact as a whole, while its structure defines the limits within which it exists and can be impacted on by the environment, but not its properties as a unity.

According to Maturana and Varela (1987), change within a specific system is determined by its structure. They distinguish two types of internal change and two types of environmental interaction.

1. Changes of state are the structural changes that a unity can undergo without a change in its organization.
2. Destructive changes are structural changes that a unity can undergo with loss of organization and therefore class identity.
3. Perturbations are interactions with the environment which trigger changes of state.
4. Destructive interactions are those that trigger destructive change.

To make it clear that change in a unity is always determined by the structure of the unity, they point out that while a lead bullet fired at point-blank range can be expected to result in destructive change to a human being it will be only a perturbation for a vampire, because of the vampire's different structure.

Maturana and Varela (1973, 1987) use the term *autopoietic systems* (from Greek words for "self" and "produce") to describe living systems, because they see them as generating and defining their own boundaries. "Living beings," say Maturana and Varela (1987), "are characterized by their autopoietic organization. They differ from each other in their structure, but they are alike in their organization" (p. 47). An autopoietic system has an autopoietic organization: it is a dynamic, closed system all of whose phenomena are subordinated to its autopoiesis. Autopoietic closure is a necessary condition for the *autonomy* of autopoietic systems. In living systems this closure is created by a continuous structural change with respect to the conditions under which matter is exchanged with the environment. Autonomy, for living systems, consists in their maintaining their organization constant in the face of continuous structural change (Maturana, 1978).

For Maturana (1978) the nervous system is a closed network of interacting neurons. A change in the activity of certain components will lead to a change in the activity of other components. Moreover, in spite of the fact that there may be surface sensory receptors, the neuronal network cannot be said to have points of entry or exit. Maturana (1983) imagines an observer in a synapse. This observer would see the presynaptic element as the effector surface and the postsynaptic element as the sensory surface, with his environment consisting of the surrounding molecules. However, the nervous system is oblivious to what the observer calls "the environment" and is affected only by the network of changing relations of activity which constitutes it.

To illustrate this point, Maturana (1978) describes a pilot flying on instruments:

The pilot is isolated from the outside world; all he can do is manipulate the instruments of the plane according . . . to the readings. When the pilot comes out of the plane, . . . his wife and friends embrace him with joy and tell him: "What a wonderful landing you made; we were afraid, because of the heavy fog." But the pilot answers in surprise: "Flight? Landing? What do you mean? I did not fly or land; I only manipulated certain internal relations of the plane in order to obtain a particular sequence of readings in a set of instruments." All that took place in the plane was determined by the structure of the plane and the pilot, and was independent of the nature of the medium that produced the perturbations [in spite of any impression an outside observer might have]. (P. 42)

When a composite unity has a structure that can change while its organization remains the same, the structural interactions that permit the organization to remain unchanged are what we have earlier referred to as *perturbations*. The structural complementarity that is necessary between a structure-determined system and its environment is called *structural coupling* (Maturana, 1983). The *ontogeny* or individual history of the living system is the history of its structural change and organizational permanence in the context of its environment. Finally, the structural congruence between the living being and its environment is called *adaptation*. When a living being maintains its adaptation, it maintains its organization (Maturana, in press).

References

Babylonian Talmud (1935). In I. Epstein (Ed. and Trans.), *Seder nezekin* (Vol. 3). London: Soncino Press.

Bateson, G. (1969/1972). The double bind. In *Steps to an ecology of mind*. New York: Ballantine.

Bateson, G. (1970/1972). Form, substance and difference. In *Steps to an ecology of mind*. New York: Ballantine.

Bateson, G. (1979). *Mind and nature: A necessary unity.* New York: E. P. Dutton.

Bateson, G., Jackson, D. D., Haley, J., & Weakland, J. H. (1956/1972). Toward a theory of schizophrenia. *Behavioral Science, 1*(4), reprinted in Bateson, G., *Steps to an ecology of mind.* New York: Ballantine.

Bertalanffy, L. von. (1968). *General system theory* (rev. ed.). New York: Braziller.

Camus, A. (1955). *The myth of Sisyphus and other essays* (J. O'Brien, Trans.). New York: Vintage/Random House.

Capra, F. (Dir.). (1946). *It's a wonderful life.* RKO/Liberty Films.

Castaneda, C. (1972). *Journey to Ixtlan.* New York: Simon & Schuster.

Cooper, D. G. (1967). *Psychiatry and antipsychiatry.* London: Tavistock.

Dell, P., & Goolishian, H. (1979). *Order through fluctuation: An evolutionary paradigm for human systems.* Paper presented at the annual scientific meeting of the A. K. Rice Institute, Houston, Texas.

Elkaïm, M. (Ed.). (1977). *Réseau—Alternative à la psychiatrie.* Paris: UGE.

Elkaïm, M. (1979). Système familial et système social. *Cahiers Critiques de Thérapie Familiale et de Pratiques de Réseaux, 1,* 55–60. Translated as Family system and social system. In M. Andolfi & I. Zwerling (Eds.), *Dimensions of Family Therapy.* New York: Guilford Press, 1980.

Elkaïm, M. (1980a). "Défamilialiser" la thérapie familiale: De l'approche familiale à l'approche socio-politique. *Cahiers Critiques de Thérapie*

Familiale et de Pratiques de Réseaux, 2, 6–16. Translated as From the family approach to the sociopolitical approach. In F. W. Kaslow (Ed.), *The international book of family therapy*. New York: Brunner/Mazel, 1980.

Elkaïm, M. (1980b). Von der Homöostase von offenen Systemen. In J. Duss-von Werdt & R. Welter-Endlin (Eds.), *Der Familienmensch*. Stuttgart: Klett-Cotta.

Elkaïm, M. (1982). Non-équilibre, hasard et changement en thérapie familiale. *Cahiers Critiques de Thérapie Familiale et de Pratiques de Réseaux*, 4–5, 55–59. Translated as Non-equilibrium, chance and change. *Journal of Marital and Family Therapy*, 7, 291–97, 1981.

Elkaïm, M. (1983). Des lois générales aux singularités. *Cahiers Critiques de Thérapie Familiale et de Pratiques de Réseaux*, 7, 111–20. Translated as From general laws to singularities. *Family Process*, 24, 151–64, 1985.

Elkaïm, M. (1985). Une approche systémique des psychothérapies de couple. In M. Elkaïm (Ed.), *Formations et pratiques en thérapie familiale*. Paris: ESF. Translated as A systemic approach to couple therapy. *Family Process*, 25, 35–42, 1986.

Elkaïm, M. (Ed.). (1987). *Les pratiques de réseau: Santé mentale et contexte social*. Paris: ESF.

Elkaïm, M., Goldbeter, A., & Goldbeter, E. (1980). Analyse des transitions de comportement dans un système familial en termes de bifurcations. *Cahiers Critiques de Thérapie Familiale et de Pratiques de Réseaux*, 3, 18–24. Translated as Analysis of the dynamics of a family system in terms of bifurcations. *Journal of Social and Biological Structures*, 10, 21–36, 1987.

Elkaïm, M., Prigogine, I., Guattari, F., Stengers, I., & Deneubourg, J.-L. (1982). Openness: A round-table discussion. *Family Process*, 21, 57–70. Translation of Prigogine, Stengers, Deneubourg, Guattari, & Elkaïm (1980).

Fivaz, E., Fivaz, R., & Kaufmann, L. (1983). Accord, conflit et symptome: Un paradigme évolutionniste. *Cahiers Critiques de Thérapie Familiale et de Pratiques de Réseaux*, 7, 91–109.

Giribone, J.-L. (1988). Quelques pas vers la contrée où les anges ont peur, in Auto-référence et Thérapie familiale (M. Elkaïm and C. Sluzki, Eds.) *Cahiers critiques de thérapie familiale et de pratiques de réseaux*, 9, 145–50.

Goldbeter, A., & Caplan, S. R. (1976). Oscillatory enzymes. *Annual Review of Biophysics and Bioengineering*, 5, 449–76.

Goldbeter, A., & Segel, L. A. (1977). Unified mechanism for relay and oscillation of cyclic AMP in Dictyostelium discoideum. *Proceedings of the National Academy of Science, 74,* 1543–47.

Guattari, F. (1979). *L'inconscient machinique: Essais de schizo-analyse.* Paris: Recherches.

Guattari, F. (1988). Les énergétiques sémiotiques. In J.-P. Brans, I. Stengers, & P. Vincke (Eds.), *Colloque de Cerisy: Temps et devenir à partir de l'oeuvre de I. Prigogine.* Geneva: Editions Patino.

Haley, J. (1959). An interactional description of schizophrenia. *Psychiatry, 22,* 321–32. Reprinted in Don D. Jackson (Ed.), (1968) *Communication, family, and marriage.* Palo Alto: Science and Behavior Books.

Homer. (1963). *The Odyssey* (R. Fitzgerald, Trans.). Garden City, N.Y.: Anchor Books/Doubleday.

Howe, R. H., & von Foerster, H. (1975). Introductory comments to Francisco Varela's Calculus for self-reference. *International Journal of General Systems, 2,* 1–3.

Jackson, D. D. (1957). The question of family homeostasis. *Psychiatric Quarterly Supplement, 31,* 79–90.

Korzybski, A. (1953). *Science and sanity.* New York: International Non-Aristotelian Library.

Laing, R. D. (1970). *Knots.* London: Tavistock.

Lettvin, J. Y., Maturana, H. R., McCulloch, W. S., & Pitts, W. H. (1959). What the frog's eye tells the frog's brain. *Proceedings of the IRE, 11,* 1940–59.

Maturana, H. R. (1975). The organization of the living: A theory of the living organization. *International Journal of Man-Machine Studies, 7,* 313–32.

Maturana, H. R. (1978). Biology of language: The epistemology of reality. In G. A. Miller & E. Lenneberg (Eds.), *Psychology and biology of language and thought.* London: Academic Press.

Maturana, H. R. (1983). What is it to see? *Archivos de Biologia y Medicina Experimentales, 16,* 255–69.

Maturana, H. R. (1990). Biologie du changement. *Cahiers Critiques de Thérapie Familiale et de Pratiques de Réseaux, 11,* 135–55.

Maturana, H. R. (in press). Biologie du phénomène social. *Cahiers Critiques de Thérapie Familiale et de Pratiques de Réseaux.*

Maturana, H. R., Uribe, G., & Frenk, S. (1968). A biological theory of relativistic colour coding in the primate retina. *Archivos de Biologia y Medicina Experimentales* (Suplemento 1).

Maturana, H. R., & Varela, F. J. (1973). *De maquinas y seres vivos.* Santiago: Editorial Universitaria.

Maturana, H. R., & Varela, F. J. (1980). *Autopoiesis and cognition.* Dordrecht: D. Reidel.

Maturana, H. R., & Varela, F. J. (1987). *The tree of knowledge: The biological roots of human understanding.* Boston: New Science Library/Shambala.

Nicolis, G. (1983). Thermodynamique de l'évolution. In Fondation Lucia de Brouckère pour la Diffusion des Sciences (Ed.), *Évolution, Connaissances du réel.* Brussels: Éditions Universitaires.

Perrault, C. (1972). *Perrault's Fairy Tales* (S. Moorsom, Trans.). Garden City, N.Y.: Doubleday.

Prigogine, I. (1977). L'ordre par fluctuations et le système social. In A. Lichnerowicz, F. Perroux, & G. Gadoffre (Eds.), *L'idée de régulation dans les sciences.* Paris: Maloine.

Prigogine, I., & Stengers, I. (1984). *Order out of chaos.* New York: Bantam.

Prigogine, I., Stengers, I., Deneubourg, J.-L., Guattari, F., & Elkaïm, M. (1980). Ouvertures. *Cahiers Critiques de Thérapie Familiale et de Pratiques de Réseaux, 3,* 7–17.

Rashi. (1949). *The Pentateuch and Rashi's commentary: Exodus* (A. Ben Isaiah & B. Sharfman, Trans.) Brooklyn, N.Y.: S. S. & R.

Rayski, A., & Courtois, S. (1987). La presse clandestine et le génocide. *Le Monde,* June 9.

Selvini Palazzoli, M., Boscolo, L., Cecchin, G., & Prata, G. (1978). *Paradox and counterparadox.* New York: Jason Aronson.

Speck, R., & Attneave, C. (1973). *Family networks.* New York: Vintage.

Sussman, M. (1964). *Growth and development.* Englewood Cliffs, N.J.: Prentice-Hall.

Varela, F. J. (1975). A calculus for self-reference. *International Journal of General Systems 2,* 5–24.

Varela, F. J. (1979). *Principles of biological autonomy.* New York: Elsevier North Holland.

Varela, F. J. (1983). L'auto-organisation: De l'apparence au méchanisme. In P. Dumouchel & J.P. Dupuy (Eds.), *Colloque de Cerisy: L'auto-organisation: De la physique au politique.* Paris: Le Seuil.

Varela, F. J. (1984). Living ways of sense-making: A middle path for neuroscience. In P. Livingston (Ed.), *Disorder and order: Proceedings of the Stanford International Symposium.* Palo Alto: Stanford, Anna Libri.

Varela, F. J. (1988). Les multiples figures de la circularité. *Cahiers critiques de thérapie familiale et de pratiques de réseaux, 9,* 45–48.

Von Foerster, H. (1984a). Disorder/order, discovery or invention. In

P. Livingston (Ed.), *Disorder and order: Proceedings of the Stanford International Symposium*. Palo Alto: Stanford, Anna Libri.

Von Foerster, H. 1984b. On constructing a reality. In W. F. E. Preiser (Ed.), *Environmental Design Research 2*. Stroudsburg, Pa.: Dowden, Hutchinson & Ross, 1973).

Von Foerster, H. (1984c). Principles of self-organization in a managerial context. In H. Ulrich & G.J.B. Probst (Eds.), *Self-organization and management of social systems*. Berlin: Springer-Verlag.

Watzlawick, P., Beavin, J. H., & Jackson, D. D. (1967). *Pragmatics of human communication*. New York: Norton.

Watzlawick, P., Weakland, J. H., & Fisch, R. (1974). *Change: Principles of problem formation and problem resolution*. New York: Norton.

Whitaker, C. A. (1975). Psychotherapy of the absurd: With a special emphasis on the psychotherapy of aggression. *Family Process, 14,* 1–16.

Whitehead, A. N., & Russell, B. (1925). *Principia mathematica* (2nd ed., Vol. 1). Cambridge: Cambridge University Press.

Index